LESTER YOUNG

Dave Gelly

Selected discography
by Tony Middleton

Spellmount
TUNBRIDGE WELLS

Hippocrene Books
NEW YORK

First published in the UK in 1984 by
SPELLMOUNT LTD
12 Dene Way, Speldhurst,
Tunbridge Wells, Kent TN3 0NX

ISBN 0 946771 06 5 (UK)

Gelly, Dave
    Lester Young. – (Jazz masters)
    1. Young, Lester   2. Jazz musicians – United States – Biography
    I. Title   II. Series
    785.42'092'4   ML 419.Y7

First published in the USA by
HIPPOCRENE BOOKS INC.
171 Madison Avenue,
New York, NY 10016

ISBN 0 87052 010 5 (USA)

Series editor: John Latimer Smith
Cover design: Peter Theodosiou

Printed & bound in Great Britain
by Anchor/Brendon Ltd, Tiptree, Essex

Contents

Acknowledgements

As far as I know, this brief sketch is the first published biography of
Lester Young. For helping me assemble the material I am deeply
indebted to Stan Britt, Brian Case, Eddie Cook, Max Jones,
Alun Morgan, Brian Priestley, Chris Sheridan, Tony Shoppee and
Spike Wells.

D.G.

The irregular combinations of fanciful invention may delight
a-while, by that novelty of which the common satiety of life sends us
all in quest; but the pleasures of sudden wonder are soon exhausted,
and the mind can only repose on the stability of truth.

SAMUEL JOHNSON: *Preface to Shakespeare*

Chapter 1

Woodville, Mississippi, is a smallish town situated roughly midway between Natchez and Baton Rouge on Highway 61, about 15 miles north of the Louisiana State Line. It has, as far as I know, only one claim to international fame and it is this: on August 27 1909 Lester Willis Young, a great American artist, was born there. It is unlikely that the Man on the Woodville Omnibus knows he ever existed. In any case, the family moved to New Orleans when Lester was an infant. We shall hear no more of Woodville.

Until well into the 1930s, rural America was roamed by minstrel shows, medicine shows, tent shows – travelling entertainments of all kinds. This was William H. (Billy) Young's business. He was leader of a carnival band which, in the manner of a circus troupe, was at least partly composed of members of the family. When a child reached a suitable age it was put to the task of learning the family trade. Billy Young could play most band instruments, though he preferred the trumpet. He could also train choirs and, although originally a blacksmith, had studied at Tuskagee Institute. A determined self-improver, he might have gone far, had he been born in another place, at another time, and a different colour.

There were six children, including Lester, his brother Lee and sister Irma. Late in his life Lester recalled being a child in New Orleans. This would have been just before and during World War I – towards the end of the great formative period of jazz in that city: 'I remember I liked to hear the music in New Orleans. I remember there were trucks advertising dances and I'd follow them around . . .'

In 1919 Mr and Mrs Young parted and Lester, Lee and Irma went with their father to Minneapolis, where Lester began his career as an apprentice musician, playing drums and doubling as handbill distributor: 'During the carnival season we all travelled with the minstrel show, through Kansas, Nebraska, South Dakota – all through there.' In between he went to school, although he never got beyond the fourth grade. 'I've been earning my own living since I was five,' he later claimed proudly, 'shining shoes, selling papers. And I was a good kid. I would *never* steal.'

He went on banging the drums and dishing out handbills until he was

13, but then gave up. 'I quit them because it was too much trouble to carry the traps and I got tired packing them up. I'd take a look at the girls after the show, and before I'd get the drums packed, they'd all gone.'

He decided to take up the less socially hampering saxophone, and it has been suggested that he made a straight swap with Lee. This would be a nice touch, since Lee was to become a well-known drummer, but it can't be true, because when Lester was 13, Lee was only five.

Billy provided an alto, taught Lester the basic fingering, and wrote out a few scales. But Lester had a very fast ear and found he could pick up the band parts easily.

'My sister was a better reader than I was . . . I always played by ear. Whatever she would play, I would play a second or third part to. One day my father spied me. He had my sister play her part and then he had me play my part alone. I couldn't play a note. He put me out of the band and wouldn't let me back in until I could read. That hurt me real bad, so I practised every day and was back in the band in about six months . . .Pretty soon I could cut everybody and I was teaching other people to read.'

One person he helped to teach was Ben Webster, who passed through Billy Young's band when Lester was in his teens: 'He used to sit and practise with me every day, and he'd try to help as much as he could.'

Honest, enterprising, helpful, with the merest leavening of cheerful indolence – this surely is a boy fit to be held up as an Example to Youth! With the addition of a cheeky grin and a fishing-rod we should have the perfect model for a Saturday Evening Post cover by Rockwell.

In fact, Lester Young was also painfully sensitive and shy. Episodes like being expelled from the family band continued to upset him, whenever he thought about them, right to the end of his life. Hostility of any kind, being shut out or rejected, caused him acute distress, and to keep these things at bay he evolved the battery of eccentricities which became his personal style as an adult: the private language, the padding gait, the aloofness, even the broad-brimmed pork-pie hat. They all said, 'I am not like you, and what you say or do cannot touch me.' His male colleagues loved him for this eccentricity; women often understood what it was in aid of. 'People think he's so cocky and secure,' Billie Holiday once said, 'but you can hurt his feelings in two seconds.' Lester's mother insisted that it was shyness that made him drink.

To make matters worse there was the question of his race. Lester was an Afro-American of mixed race, with lightish features, green eyes and auburn hair. (In later life he wore his hair straightened, or 'conked', which darkened it. When a conk was wearing off the auburn tinge would come back. It was easy to get Lester hopping mad; you just had to call him 'Red'.)

Born and raised in the South, he knew how things stood, but it took a small occurrence to make him feel personally oppressed for the first time. With Irma, he went to church in some small town where the carnival had stopped. The congregation was mainly white and the preacher, in full spate, was making their flesh creep as he warned them that their 'black sins' would find them out, that they would be cast into the pit of everlasting damnation – the 'blackest hell of all.' The implication sank in.

The break with the Young family band came finally in the fall of 1927, when they were in Salina, Kansas. Billy Young announced that he was going to take them South for the winter, through Texas and on into the Deep South. Unwilling to face the unpleasantness and indignity of a Southern tour, Lester pleaded with his father to stay around Kansas, Nebraska and Iowa. There was plenty of work, he pointed out, and there would be far less trouble. Billy Young didn't want to endure winter in the mid-West and refused to consider the idea. The band left and Lester stayed.

He joined a local band, Art Bronson's Bostonians, on baritone saxophone, and it was with Bronson that he at last began playing the instument which was to give voice to his genius – the tenor saxophone. The band's regular tenor player was a moneyed dilettante who turned up only when he felt like it. Lester offered to take the job on if Bronson would fire the man. From now on, Lester played the tenor, and his name began to be passed around among travelling musicians as a young man to look out for. This would be around 1929–30. The chronology of Lester's early career is hopelessly tangled. No-one in his circle kept diaries, he never signed contracts or got noticed in the press. Jazz activity in the South- and Mid-West, known as the 'Territory', was a boiling stew, with players moving from band to band, bands forming and collapsing, all against a background of prohibition and a gangster-controlled entertainment business.

Nevertheless, it is fairly certain that, on leaving Bronson, Lester joined the New Orleans pioneer King Oliver, then in his declining years. 'He was old then,' Lester recalled (in fact, Oliver was only about 46), 'and he didn't play all night, but his tone was full when he played.'

11

Oliver was suffering from the gum disease which finally put an end to his playing career.

After King Oliver, Lester drifted around, occasionally returning to Minneapolis, which he regarded as home. There he joined a touring band called the Blue Devils, led by bass player Walter Page. Page was a splendid player, later the pivot of Count Basie's matchless rhythm section, but he was an unlucky bandleader.

'The Blue Devils band was getting bruised, I mean really bruised,' said Lester. 'One time our instruments were impounded in West Virginia and they took us to the railroad track and told us to get out of town.' Some hobos showed them how to jump aboard a moving train and they managed to get as far as Cincinnati. They decided there that it was every man for himself ('every tub on its own bottom', as the saying was) and split up.

Lester found his way back to Minneapolis and got a job in the band at the Cotton Club there. After work he would listen to the radio, particularly to a nightly live broadcast by the Count Basie band from the Reno Club, Kansas City. He loved the sound, the approach, the rhythm section, but couldn't bear the tenor player. Acting on a thoroughly uncharacteristic impulse, he sent Basie a telegram. The text of it is unknown; Basie remembered it as being 'strange and convincing'. He had, anyhow, heard of Lester on the musicians' grapevine and sent for him. 'It was very nice,' said Lester. 'Just like I thought it would be.'

Lester made few decisive or forceful moves in his life, but every one was crucial: he had refused to follow his father to Texas, he had shoved Bronson's tenor player aside so that he could get to play the instrument himself, now he had invited himself into Basie's band – perhaps the only one in the world where his extraordinary talent could be nurtured and stretched.

We have only the enthusiastic but vague words of those who heard him at the time (modified, in any case, by hindsight) to tell us exactly how Lester was playing when he arrived in Kansas City. When and how his individuality first revealed itself is even harder to discover, but it was certainly there in his choice of models.

His was the first generation of jazz musicians to get its early influences from records. Men only ten years or so older, such as Armstrong, couldn't have done this because there *were* no jazz records to speak of before about 1920. Lester's ear was caught by the sounds of two saxophonists in particular, Frankie Trumbauer and Jimmy Dorsey.

Publicity photograph for Norman Granz's JATP (Verve Records)

'They were the only ones telling a story I liked to hear . . . Trumbauer always told a little story. And I liked the way he slurred the notes . . . Did you ever hear him play *Singing The Blues*? That tricked me right then, and that's where I went.'

Trumbauer played the C-melody saxophone, a variety now extinct, pitched higher than the tenor but lower than the alto. His sound has a fragile, keening quality to it, almost devoid of vibrato, and his articulation is very precise. No-one would claim a place for Trumbauer in the jazz pantheon, but on records such as *Singing The Blues*, *Wringing And Twisting* and *For No Reason At All In C*, with Bix Beiderbecke, he creates attractive, slightly whimsical little solos of some charm.

These records came out in 1928, when Lester was 18 or 19; the very first Trumbauer he is likely to have heard is on records by the Sioux City Six, issued in 1924. In view of Lester's temperament, the strikingly light, contained tone which musicians recalled hearing in Kansas City, and on the evidence of his playing when he finally began making records, Trumbauer is entirely credible as an influence. When Lester was a boy, in the Twenties, he was not playing an instrument with a tradition of great jazz performers. Most saxophone players habitually produced either a kind of rubbery belch or a low, mooing noise. It was not an encouraging instrument for a young man to find himself struggling with. Amidst all the surrounding hooting and gargling, Trumbauer's precision and restraint must have been irresistibly attractive.

It is perfectly possible to hear echoes in Lester's playing of his early liking for Trumbauer: the sudden rip up to an isolated high note, the little scooping inflexions, the curiously 'floating' quality of sound, which Lester shared with no other known saxophonist, until people began imitating his own records. Lester Young is an infinitely greater artist than Frankie Trumbauer, and the influence gradually faded throughout Lester's career, but to suggest, as some critics have, that he was kidding when he acknowledged Trumbauer is nonsense.

There is, of course, the inconvenient fact that Trumbauer was white. Lester, who managed throughout his life to infuriate authoritative and tidy-minded people simply by going quietly about his business, achieved a masterpiece here. According to the rules, black jazz musicians influence white ones and, to be honest, this is almost invariably the case. But, by blandly claiming Trumbauer as his first master, Lester implied that it doesn't *have* to be the case. Indeed, it is quite possible that, as he played his Trumbauer records on his portable phonograph, he had no idea whether the man was black, white or, like himself, a bit of both.

In 1933 – around the time Lester first joined Basie in Kansas City – ten per cent of the city's police force had known criminal records. This entertaining little statistic points to the fact that it was what used to be called a 'wide open town'. Run for a decade and a half by a gangster-politician named Tom Pendergast, Kansas City had more dives, brothels, gin-mills, dancehalls, cabarets and gambling tables than anywhere else. 'With the possible exception of Singapore and Port Said,' the District Attorney remarked, 'Kansas City has the greatest sin industry in the world.' Situated at the confluence of two major rivers and the junction of seven main railroad lines, it was the business centre of the West – and what could be more pleasant after a day's hard dealing than a little fun and games, with no pettifogging restrictions to dampen the proceedings?

Like New Orleans in the early years of the century, Kansas City – 'Kaycee' – in the 1930s has passed into jazz history as a species of Elysium, largely through the recollections of musicians who worked there at the time. Even allowing for the softening effect of nostalgia, it must have been a remarkable place, with its prodigious nightlife and non-stop jam-sessions. The hours were long (it has been estimated that Basie's men averaged 60 hours a week) and the pay terrible, but standards were ferociously high. At after-hours jam-sessions players challenged one another in feats of imaginative agility that could go on until mid-morning. Touring musicians, passing through town, could get badly burned in these contests, as pianist Mary Lou Williams recalled:

> 'The word went round that Hawkins was in the Cherry Blossom, and within about half an hour there were Lester Young, Ben Webster, Herschel Evans, Herman Walder, and one or two unknown tenors piling into the club to blow.
> 'Bean (Hawkins) didn't know the Kaycee tenor men were so terrific, and he couldn't get himself together though he played all morning. I happened to be nodding that night, and around 4am I awoke to hear someone pecking on my screen.
> 'I opened the window on Ben Webster. He was saying, "Get up, Pussycat, we're jammin' and all the pianists are tired out now.

Hawkins has got his shirt off and he's still blowing. You got to come down!"

'Sure enough, when we got there, Hawkins was in his singlet, taking turns with the Kaycee men. It seems he had run into something he didn't expect.

'Lester's style was light and, as I said, it took him maybe five choruses to warm up. But then he would really blow; then you couldn't handle him on a cutting session.

'That was how Hawkins got hung up. The Henderson band was playing in St Louis that evening, and Bean knew he ought to be on the way. But he kept trying to blow something to beat Ben and Herschel and Lester. When at last he gave up, he got straight in his car and drove to St Louis. I heard he'd just bought a new Cadillac and he burnt it out trying to make the job on time. Yes, Hawkins was king until he met those crazy Kansas City tenor men.'

The story of the Routing of Hawkins is one of the great myths of jazz, taking 'myth' in the sense of 'a tale concerning heroes, handed down by tradition from antiquity'. If it isn't literally true in all its details (the singlet, the Cadillac, the epic length of the session), it represents, in emblematic form, all that Kaycee stood for.

And Kaycee musicians took the jam-sessions with them when they themselves went on tour. Buddy Tate, interviewed by Russell Davies for a BBC radio programme about Lester, remembered one night in Tulsa, Oklahoma:

'Down in the lobby of the hotel where we were staying they had a piano, and musicians used to come in and jam. And someone says, "Lester's upstairs." So I thought, I think I'll go wake him up, make him play some! . . . I went up to his room and he says, "Oh, really! Well wait. Can you wait till I get my clothes on?" He just *loved* to play. And he just jumped into his clothes right quick and came downstairs and started to blowing. Man, I shall always remember the sounds that came out of that horn!'

With Basie, Lester played at the Reno club, by Kansas City standards a fairly elaborate joint. It had a floor show, with a compere, a song-and-patter man, a comedienne, and one Christine Buckner, billed as 'the world's fastest dancer'. The bandstand was so small that Basie's piano had to stand on the floor, and there was a hole cut in the shell over the stage to accommodate the double bass. It is said that Lester acquired his curious way of holding the saxophone – at an angle of 45 degrees – at the Reno, because that was the only way he could keep it from banging into someone else's instrument. I doubt whether this is true. More likely it was one of his many little oddities and affectations, but it went well with his sidelong phrasing, and indeed with his approach to life in general.

Basie's band soon gained a great reputation in Kansas City, where reputations were not easy to earn. There was even a little balcony above the bandstand for people who had come just for the music. They could also get high at no extra charge, simply by breathing in the marajuana fumes rising from the stage.

By 1934 Lester's work with Basie and his jam-session exploits had spread his name among touring musicians right across America. Many had not actually heard him, because he had, as yet, made no records, but it was common knowledge that in Kaycee there was a shy, peculiar young man whom it was unwise to engage in a battle of musical wits.

Among those who *had* heard him was the bandleader Fletcher Henderson. He had been captivated by Lester's playing, so much so that when the great Coleman Hawkins announced that he was leaving to take up an offer of work in Europe, Henderson offered his place to Lester. The offer was immensely flattering, but Lester was enjoying himself so much in Kaycee that he was in two minds about accepting. Basie told him to go ahead and grab the chance while he had it, so Lester left to join Henderson in New York. It was a move he was soon to regret. Lester. The proposition was immensely flattering, but Lester was enjoying himself so much in Kaycee that he was in two minds about accepting. Basie told him to go ahead and grab the chance while he had it, so Lester left to join Henderson in New York. It was a move he was soon to regret.

Henderson's orchestra was a star attraction and changes in its personnel were carefully noted in the entertainment pages of the black press. The Chicago Defender of April 14 1934 announced: 'Two new men have joined the Henderson band, Elmer James, bass player, and Lester Young of Kansas City, one of the most celebrated tenor sax players in the music world.' One should not read too much into this. The phrase is a piece of slack journalese (What other world *would* a tenor sax player be celebrated in?), stuck in to fill out an otherwise bald paragraph. But attention of this kind made Lester nervously aware that his debut would be watched critically by far more people than the nightly clientele at the Reno club.

It soon became obvious that something was wrong. The Henderson saxophone section, used to the broad, sweeping tone of Hawkins, simply swallowed Lester's sound. It was as if he wasn't there at all. No-one could fault his sight-reading or general musicianship, but there just wasn't *enough* of him. The musicians muttered among themselves, made acid comments, pointedly ignored him. Lester's worst nightmares was coming true; he was the centre of hostile attention, shut out, humiliated in public. It was like being sent away from the family band all over again, but a thousand times worse.

Henderson's wife, Leora, a strong-minded woman and something of a power behind the throne, decided to do something. She began giving Lester a crash course in Coleman Hawkins. She woke him up in the morning to Hawkins records, she chivvied him around music shops in search of reeds and mouthpieces that would put flesh on his tone, she scolded him brightly, in the manner of a ward-sister with a recalcitrant patient. No doubt she meant well, but to the end of his life Lester would refer to Leora only as 'that bitch, Henderson's wife'.

It was hopeless, and an end had to be called. Before speaking to Lester, Henderson addressed the rest of the saxophone section. 'I'm going to let this boy go,' he said, 'because he'll have no peace around here. But before I do, I just want to say this: he can outplay you – and you – and *you*!'

The condemned man made one last request, a letter from Henderson stating that he had not been fired. He would never have to show it to a prospective employer, but that wasn't the point. On paper, at least, he had not been thrown out.

Disconsolately, he took a job with Andy Kirk's Clouds of Joy for a while and, as soon as he could, went back to Basie at the Reno Club. The Henderson episode was never mentioned.

The Reno had a direct link with the Kansas City radio station, W9XBY, which regularly plugged into the link to provide late-night dance music for its listeners. W9XBY was a small station, but it had an exceptionally powerful transmitter. In the early hours of the morning, when most local stations had closed down, leaving the airwaves clear, it could be picked up hundred of miles away.

John Hammond, critic, entrepreneur and avid jazz-lover, has told the story innumerable times of how he first heard Basie's band, twiddling the dial of his car radio at 1am in a Chicago parking lot. He was instantly captivated, particularly by the purity and economy of Basie's piano style. 'With fewer notes he was saying all that Waller and Hines could say pianistically, using perfectly timed punctuations – a chord, even a single note – which could inspire a horn player to heights he had never reached before.' It was in exactly the same circumstances, over W9XBY in the early hours, that Lester had recognised the same quality – and decided to send off his famous telegram.

For Hammond, hearing something that excited him was enough to set him vigorously in motion. He determined to do something about the Basie band. He began to write glowingly about Basie in 'Down Beat' and elsewhere, and to bend every available ear on the subject of the obscure little group in Kansas City. As soon as he could he set out for Kaycee and the Reno Club. It was everything he had hoped for, and more. He stayed on until the club closed and then accompanied Lester on his early-morning prowl in search of a jam-session, which they found at a joint on 18th Street, where pianist Clarence Johnson was installed.

Returning in high excitement to New York, Hammond convinced the American Record Company that Basie would be just the thing for their Brunswick label. He negotiated what he thought was a pretty good deal, including royalty payments, which it was unusual for bands to get in those days, and returned to Kansas City with the draft contract for Basie to sign.

Basie greeted him warmly. 'Your friend was here, John,' he said.

'What friend? I didn't send anybody.'

'Fellow called Dave Kapp. Said he was representing you and gave me the contract to sign.'

Kapp, head of Decca Records, had got there first and, more important, got Basie to sign what Hammond later described as a 'slave contract' – $750 for 24 sides, each year for three years, and no royalty.

Hammond blamed himself for letting his enthusiasm run away with him and telling all and sundry about Basie before taking care of business. Nevertheless, it did result in the MCA booking corporation signing Basie to a management contract. Basie was to leave Kansas City immediately, to become a nationally promoted attraction.

Chapter 2

En route for New York and the Decca studios, the Basie band were booked for a short season at the Grand Terrace Cafe in Chicago. This was their first trip away from the Territory, the beginning of the climb to the big time – although onlookers might not have believed it.

Enlarged from nine to thirteen pieces, the orchestra wasn't exactly the kind of outfit to make socialites swoon with delight. In fact it was rough. In Reno Club days the band's entire library of music was kept in an old briefcase; most of the numbers consisted of riffs superimposed on other riffs and interspersed with solos. A nine-piece band was small enough to work like this without arrangements; a nod, a signal, a *sotto voce* phrase was all that was needed to set the whole thing going. Even with thirteen it's perfectly possible, but they need to know each other well. Also, you can play riffs using this method, but nothing more ambitious, and from now on Basie was going to need some more elaborate arrangements. Fletcher Henderson lent him a few, to get through the opening weeks – and then there was the special music provided for accompanying the Show.

'Remembering those first nights at the Grand Terrace,' said John Hammond, 'I am astonished that they weren't fired.' Half the band were poor sight-readers and faked along like Polar explorers roped together, hoping to God the man in front wasn't lost too. It was probably the chorus girls who saved them because, whatever cacophony was going on in the horn department, Jo Jones's drums provided the best dancing rhythm they had ever known – and they said so.

It was in Chicago that John Hammond was able to have some small revenge on Decca for pinching Basie from under his nose. He was determined to get in first and record at least some of the band before they got to New York. He fixed up a session featuring Buck Clayton on trumpet and Lester Young on tenor, with the Basie-Page-Jones rhythm section. At the last minute Buck Clayton fell victim to the trumpet player's occupational injury, a split lip, so his section-mate Carl 'Tatti' Smith came along instead. The date was October 9 1936, the time 10 o'clock in the morning – before the musicians retired to bed.

Forty-five years later, after a lifetime as a record producer, Hammond could still say, quite categorically, 'It's the only perfect, *completely* perfect recording session I've ever had anything to do with.' It was Lester Young's first recording, the first time his music was caught and frozen into shellac grooves and sent out into the world. He never surpassed his performance on *Lady Be Good* and *Shoe Shine Swing*, two of the four pieces recorded at the session. Listening to them today, it takes not the slightest effort of historical imagination to experience again the thrill that stayed with John Hammond for half a century.

What is so special about it? Well, ignoring technicalities for the moment, there is first of all the same feeling of bursting life and blazing energy that one gets with Armstrong during the Hot Five period (when, incidentally, he was the same age as Lester was when he made this first record). It derives from the confidence and poise of a young man who is aware of his powers and in full control of them. Lester's tone, articulation, rhythmic control and melodic vocabulary had all come to a point of perfect balance some time back in Kansas City; what we have here is the work of his early maturity.

When you consider all the negligible stuff that got recorded, even in the depths of the Depression, it is maddening to reflect that no-one had the wit to record Lester Young until 1936. I would willingly swap, for instance, the entire output of the Casa Loma Orchestra for one session by Lester in 1934 or '35.

However, the first was Chicago 1936, and the first thing they played was *Shoe Shine Swing* (actually the old Cahn-Chaplin ditty *Shoe Shine Boy*), of which there are two extant takes. Nothing becomes Lester's recorded career so well as his first utterance – a phrase eight bars long, starting and finishing with exactly the same interval (C to F in quavers) and packed with his own brand of devious candour. The notes themselves are perfectly straightforward; all but two of them are contained in the scale of F major. And if you wrote it down you'd end up with eight bars of harmless-looking crotchets and quavers, not even a triplet to disturb things. So why, when you try to hum it or whistle it, does it take half a dozen goes to get it right? There are moments during this solo when I could swear that Lester stops and winks. Three times he ends a phrase with a sly little droop from D flat to C, and then pauses. 'Uh-huh!'

This teasing and deceptive simplicity drove other musicians either wild with delight or mad with outrage. The outraged ones were usually saxophone players of the more ornate variety, who took it as a personal affront when somebody who didn't know how to hold the instrument

Lester Young with Benny Goodman, late 1930s (Melody Maker)

properly came on playing solos with notes only one step more complicated than bugle calls in a tone that was – well, what was it exactly?

You do need a certain amount of historical imagination to understand the furore caused in saxophonic circles by Lester's tone. Henderson's men weren't alone in being scandalised. When the first records came out they were so unexpected in every way that people who didn't like them settled on the most obvious characteristic, the sound, to be scathing and witty about. It was pale, it was limp, it sounded like a gaspipe etc etc. In fact, what they really meant was it didn't sound like Coleman Hawkins.

Hawkins had, to all intents and purposes, invented the tenor saxophone as a jazz instrument. For the past seven years his beefy sound and urgent, snapping phrases had been the standard by which all other players were judged. His reputation as a great master had taken him to Europe, where tenor players had treated him with the same awed respect which classical cellists accorded Pablo Casals. There was majesty in Hawkins's playing, informed by a mind and an ear so comprehensive that the idea of anyone ever challenging him seemed laughable.

Hawkins's method was to push hard, pressing every drop of harmonic juice out of a theme. He took tunes apart, brushing aside the simple harmonies provided by their composers and erecting in their place a dense forest of substitutions, additions and passing chords. When a Hawkins solo finishes you half expect to hear him say, 'There, that's a bit more like it. Now, what else have you got to show me?' The grandeur of his conception was expressed through a tone not only broad but biting. It had what saxophonists call 'edge'.

By contrast, Lester's tone had no edge at all. It didn't cut, it floated. Some commentators, perhaps drawing an analogy with vocal techniques, have declared that, whereas Hawkins blew from the diaphragm, Lester seemed to produce his tone from his chest. This is not so. Anyone who has ever tried playing the tenor saxophone knows that you can't make any kind of sound by just using the chest muscles. Lester's tone was supported by just as much air as Hawkins's. Indeed, listening to *Shoe Shine Swing*, one has the impression that the process started somewhere in the region of his boots.

The fact is that Lester's sound was inseparable from his thoughts, just as Hawkins's was from his. We shall see later that as his melodic ideas changed, so did his tone.

Before leaving the subject of Lester's tone for the time being, one aspect must be mentioned, because it occurs in *Shoe Shine Swing* – his exploitation of the mechanics of his instrument to create varying densities of sound. The saxophone has an effective range of two and a half octaves (if we ignore, as Lester did, the high harmonics, or 'freak notes'). Roughly half-way up this compass the player as it were changes gear. Having raised all the keys, he depresses his left thumb, engaging a mechanism which splits the air column, and starts again at the bottom. There is an overlap between these two registers, and several notes can be played with two totally different fingerings. However, one fingering produces an 'open' and one a 'closed' sound. By alternating the two Lester was able to repeat a single note with two distinct sonorities – 'mm-aah'. Added to his habit of playing ear-deceiving rhythmic patterns, this effect could be quite magical.

But there is more to it than that. The two registers have distinct sonorities in any case, especially around the 'break', where the gear-change occurs. Academically trained players work hard to eliminate this difference in the interests of even tone production, but Lester had not experienced the dubious benefits of academic training. He had noticed that the lower closed notes produced a reverberant, honking sound and developed their use to great expressive effect. Bars 25 to 28 of his first chorus on *Shoe Shine Swing* present us with a classic example. They consist entirely of the honking closed D (middle C on the piano) and the bland B (piano A). The stress always falls on the D, a taut, booming note, adding significantly to the rhythmic tension of the whole solo.

Leaving Chicago and the Grand Terrace, the Basie men made their way, playing one-night stands, through blizzard-torn New England to Buffalo and thence to New York City. They opened at the Roseland Ballroom in November.

This place has now come to represent the Good Old Days for many Americans, perhaps because it's one of the few remnants of their earlier popular culture they haven't either knocked down or converted into a theme-park. In point of fact, when Basie played there it was a taxi-dance hall ('Come on, big boy, ten cents a dance'), with a rigid whites-only policy. As Lester would put it, it was a 'crow joint'. Roseland, we are told, was better than most because the band could play whole numbers. In other taxi halls no tune was allowed to run longer than 90 seconds, because time was money to the girls. Still, as André Gide cheeringly remarked, in a somewhat different context, art thrives on constraint and dies in freedom.

The band's reception was decidedly mixed. John Hammond had been enthusing wildly about Basie for months, and he was an influential and respected man. He wrote columns in both the American and British musical press, and his judgment was regarded as infallible. As a result, Basie's opening night presented the interesting spectacle of show-business writers and entertainment personalities buying rolls of dance tickets at the paybox in order to hear what all the fuss was about.

On the whole they weren't impressed, and it's not difficult to see why. The swing era was getting into its full stride; big bands, both black and white, were becoming slicker and more elaborate as they competed for the attention of the growing audience. Section work was drilled to West Point standard, dynamics shifted subtly, like the gears of a new Cadillac, and everything was on show. And here were these thirteen funky characters, straight out of a Kaycee rathole, who didn't seem to realise that this was New York City, where you have to be slick or you're nothing.

In later years Basie was fond of quoting one of their first reviews: 'If you think the saxes are out of tune, listen to the brass. And if you think the brass is out of tune, listen to the whole band!' Of course, since Roseland was a crow joint, most of the people really qualified to judge were excluded anyway.

But listen to the first Basie recordings, made in January 1937, alongside any of the established bands of the period – Henderson, Goodman, Lunceford – and you can see what the trouble was. Judged by the criteria which they regarded as essential, Basie's band was a non-starter.

The very first tune recorded by the full band was Fats Waller's *Honeysuckle Rose*, and it's as good an example as any of the Basie method. Basie plays two choruses on piano, the first sticking close to the melody, in simple but fully voiced stride style; Lester enters with a two-bar break, effecting a key change, and takes a high-spirited chorus, not quite in the *Shoe Shine Swing* class but elegant nonetheless. By now we're more than half-way through the record and the full band hasn't played a note yet. The sections come in for just two choruses, superimposed riffs with the middle-eights left open – the first for the rhythm section and the second for Tatti Smith. And that's it.

The earliest Basie records are fascinating in that they have two distinct types of arrangement – the loose, KC riff kind as described above, and the full orchestrations that the band was adding as quickly as possible. The former are still fresh and exciting, while the latter have grown a little quaint with the passing years. It took some time, maybe as long as two years, before this awkward duality was finally resolved and Basie's arrangers, notably Eddie Durham, Buck Clayton and Jimmy Munday, achieved a written style as easy-sounding and flexible as the head arrangements.

Trombonist Dickie Wells, describing his audition before joining Basie in 1938, provides a wonderful insider's account of the band at work during this period in his book 'The Night People':

'Come on,' Basie said, 'take your axe out and sit down and blow with the cats. See if you like it.'

'Where's my music?' I asked.

'Sit in and see what happens,' he said . . .

Basie would start out and vamp a little, set a tempo and call out, 'That's it!' He'd set a rhythm for the saxes first and Earle Warren would pick that up and lead the saxes. Then he'd set one for the bones and we'd pick that up. Now it's our rhythm against theirs. The third rhythm would be for the trumpets and they'd start fanning their Derbies . . .

The solos would fall between the ensembles, but that's how the piece would begin, and that's how Basie put his tunes together. He had a big band, but he handled it as though it were six pieces.

'Am I hired?' I asked him.

'I didn't fire you, did I?' was his answer.

What Basie was doing was saving the swing era from itself by insisting on the basic premise, essential to jazz, that the music must start with the musicians themselves and their individual styles. The Count Basie Orchestra was not 'a thirteen-piece band', it was those particular thirteen men. Change one and you change the whole thing. Ellington and Basie were different in almost every respect, but in this fundamental matter they were identical.

When the band left Roseland and played at the Savoy Ballroom and the Apollo Theatre in Harlem it was greeted ecstatically. The black audience understood it in a way in which white people were only just

27

learning to. Hammond was exceptional in that he had an instant feeling for black music. Indeed, he was always rather put out when other white people couldn't hear what he could hear, and had a missionary's zeal to lead them to the light. They usually rewarded him with remarks like, 'Yes, John, but it'll never go in Philadelphia.'

The Count Basie Orchestra, as it settled down in its first four years, enlarged to fourteen, consisted of: Ed Lewis, Buck Clayton and Harry Edison (trumpets), Dickie Wells, Benny Morton and Dan Minor (trombones), Earle Warren (alto saxophone), Lester Young and Herschel Evans (tenor saxophones), Jack Washington (baritone saxophone), Count Basie (piano), Freddie Greene (guitar), Walter Page (bass), Jo Jones (drums) – with Jimmy Rushing and Helen Humes as vocalists.

A strange, exasperated friendship grew between Lester and Herschel Evans, as is often the case when two utterly different people are thrown together by circumstance. Herschel came from Texas, and Texan tenor players have, for generations, been identifiable for their huge tone and melodramatic style of expression. Nothing could have been further from Lester's light, wry, mercurial way of playing, and Herschel was Lester's opposite in character, too. Lester was always worried about hurting people's feelings, always padding around the edge of an argument before joining in. Herschel normally started with a stream of insults; if the victim took it in good part, he was okay.

The whole relationship, both musical and personal, is summed up in a single exchange, recounted years later by Billie Holiday:

Herschel: Why don't you go buy an alto, man? You only got an alto tone.

Lester (tapping his forehead): There's things going on up here, man. Some of you guys are all belly.

They were forever at it, and nobody knew when they were being serious and when they were kidding.

Herschel joined the band just before it left Kansas City, and Basie immediately realised the musical drama inherent in these opposed styles and temperaments: the Battle of the Tenors, a cutting contest, a nightly event – like a prizefight, at least three-quarters flim-flam – but they played their parts with relish.

Herschel would open with his customary wheezing roar, notes smearing all over the place, greasy Texas blues. Lester's entry would be extra-fastidious, each phrase articulated with pointed delicacy and the ghost of a sneer. They used to do it regularly on *One O'Clock Jump* – ostentatiously turning their backs on each other.

They would never admit it, but they thought the world of one another. According to other members of the band, Lester was inconsolable when Herschel died in 1939, at the age of 30.

The years between 1936 and 1941 were golden ones for Lester Young. It may have taken him a long time to get recorded in the first place, but once the Basie band started making records he was in and out of the studios constantly. Also, this was the great era of live broadcasting from hotels, nightclubs and ballrooms. That is how Hammond heard Basie in the first place – and now the band's music, hours of it, was pouring out through radio transmitters in the early hours. From February 1937 until he left Basie in December 1940, Lester's tenor can be heard soloing on every broadcast and record session, hundreds of titles, and more still turn up from time to time, when some small radio station has a clear-out and discovers a pile of old acetate transcriptions.

As a body of work it is astonishingly consistent, so much so that to pick out the best is an impossible task. He claimed in later years that his favourite solo on a Basie record was *Taxi War Dance*. The title is a pun on 'taxi dance', à la Roseland, and 'taxi war' a New York cab drivers' dispute that was raging at the time. In form, the piece is in the old Basie style – solos followed by riffs – and Lester's chorus comes right at the beginning. Opening with a twisted quotation from *Ol' Man River*, he jumps in as though propelled by powerful elastic. The harmonic sequence is slightly more complicated than *Shoe Shine Swing*, being, in effect, a truncated version of the ballad *Willow Weep For Me*. The way he flips lightly through the chord changes, touching each one deftly while carving an elegant and energetic line, puts one in mind of a gymnast or ballet dancer. Rudolf Nureyev once said that a great dancer is not one who makes a difficult step look easy but one who makes an easy step look interesting. Lester contrives to do both at once. He twists lazily through the difficult parts and arrives at the easy final cadence, a simple dominant-to-tonic, at the last possible moment, with a negligent little bounce.

The entire solo is thirty-two bars long; it takes exactly 35 seconds, and it's a masterpiece to stand alongside Armstrong's *West End Blues* and Parker's *Ko-Ko*. No-one else could have done it because no-one else's mind worked that way. The thought and its expressions are one and instantaneous, and that is what makes jazz unique in Western

John Lewis, Aaron Bell, Lester Young & Jesse Drakes at Birdland in the late 1940s (Melody Maker)

music.

As an improvising musician, Lester had always chafed somewhat at the restrictions of orchestral playing. For long periods he would be functioning simply as a member of the saxophone section. Unleashed, he would produce 16 or 32 bars of solo in a concentrated burst and subside once more into the section. It is the very constriction which gives the solos their unique force, a sense of endless possibilities briefly glimpsed.

His solos with Basie occur almost exclusively in mid- to up-tempo numbers. It was here that his lithe muscularity, supported by the matchless spring of Basie's rhythm section, showed up most effectively against the weight of the full orchestra. In ballads, such as *Blue And Sentimental*, it was Herschel, with his blowsy romanticism, who came to the fore.

But Lester had another, concurrent career at this time. Away from the band he revealed a side of his musical personality that someone who had only heard him playing with Basie would never have suspected. It is to be found in the chamber music of the swing era, small groups of soloists from the big bands. In the years 1937 to 1940 Lester Young recorded regularly with these informal little bands and some of his finest work is captured on records by the Kansas City Six and Seven, a single session by the Benny Goodman Septet and, in particular, a collection of pieces featuring Billie Holiday which have long been acknowledged as pinnacles of the jazz art.

The Lester who emerges in these works is an artist of transparent delicacy. Relieved of the necessity to project his sound through the mass of the orchestra, and of fashioning his line so that it forms a seamless join with the arrangement, he becomes reflective and conversational. The mere reduction in volume (and, for all his lightness, his solos with the orchestra must have been quite loud) imparts intimacy to his tone, and he is able to bring into play a whole new vocabulary of inflection and minute timing.

On September 27 1938 a group of Basie musicians recorded, under the name of the Kansas City Six, for the Commodore label, an offshoot of the Commodore Record Shop, one of the first stores catering to the emerging specialist jazz market. Very occasionally the atmosphere of a recording session is caught on a record, along with the music. One thinks of Thelonious Monk's first *Round Midnight*, Parker's *Loverman* or

Clifford Brown's Paris sessions as examples. The Kansas City Six records have that quality, in this case a palpable aura of relaxed well-being. The six players were easy in each other's company, they knew one another's playing intimately, the affair had been arranged by Commodore's proprietor, Milt Gabler, who was a fan. Everybody felt like settling down to a few hours' playing. It was a perfect set-up and it produced perfect results.

The six were: Buck Clayton, trumpet; Lester Young, tenor saxophone and clarinet; Freddie Greene, guitar; Walter Page, bass; Jo Jones, drums – and trombonist Eddie Durham, playing his other instrument, the electric guitar. They played five numbers, two takes of each: *Way Down Yonder In New Orleans, Countless Blue, Them There Eyes, I Want A Little Girl* and *Pagin' The Devil*.

The first thing one notices about the tenor saxophone solos is their remarkable combination of reticence and energy. Lester is obviously playing at about half the volume he used with Basie, but closer to the microphone. Some of his notes are mere whispers; one can hear the free air around them as he half voices them. With the orchestra, all that air would have been pushed against the reed to carry the sound. And yet the line is as taut as ever, firmly articulated and moving with faultless logic.

One can't help noticing either that, when he was at his happiest and most buoyant, Lester played predominantly in the higher register of the saxophone, relishing the tonal ambiguities of the octave-break, and playing repeated rhythmic patterns on the closed D and E flat (piano C and D flat). He seems to derive a childlike delight from the physical sensation of these notes as they reverberate along the full length of the instrument.

It is with such small-group recordings that one is struck by the full force of Lester's originality, an originality which becomes the more astonishing as one appreciates again the simplicity of means by which it is expressed.

Reputable histories of jazz have customarily laid great stress on harmonic innovation as a crucial determinant of stylistic change, representing it as a process of complication through Hawkins to Parker, a sudden and decisive turn to a new simplicity with Miles Davis's 'modal' style and, in turn, an elaboration of this into melodic lines derived from harmonies built on fourths, or from no harmonies at all. This is a perfectly reasonable analysis, and it reveals the undoubted truth that jazz has traced in less than a century roughly the same harmonic path as European concert music – Baroque, Classical, Romantic, Impressionist, Atonal.

But Lester Young doesn't fit into this thesis. He was beyond question a radical and original thinker and, even if by delayed action, massively influential. Unlike Monk, he didn't create a sealed-off style which few were tempted to emulate, or gather around him a tiny school of acolytes, like Lennie Tristano. He stands firmly in the mainstream of jazz history, and yet, as Benny Green so neatly puts it, he 'did nothing to corrupt the harmonic innocence of his times.'

What he did was to see shapes in innocent harmonies that no-one else could see, until he showed them. He made an earth-bound chord float weightlessly by emphasising notes which other players regarded as secondary – the ninth over a dominant seventh, the sixth over a minor triad, the softly romantic augmented fifth. And always there is the minute adjustment of tonal weight, trimming and balancing note against note and phrase against phrase. Exegesis along European academic lines has the equipment to deal with Parker's harmonic discoveries, but it is helpless when faced with two bars of straight crotchets on the tonic note, each one subtly different from the others. You can't write that down on manuscript paper, you have to hear it.

It is on the Kansas City Six records also that we have the best examples of Lester's clarinet playing. It was not an instrument to which he had devoted much time. Saxophone players were required to 'double' on clarinet in the thirties and forties, just as nowadays they are expected to turn their hands to the flute. Typically, Lester had acquired an oddity on which to perform his clarinet duties. It was a metal instrument, intended for robust use with military bands, and from it he produced a sound unlike anyone else's, plangent and curiously hollow.

Whereas the tenor saxophone seems to be a part of him, the clarinet is clearly a stranger and he treats it, as was his way with strangers, with inquisitive circumspection. Careful and tentative, Lester's clarinet playing has a disarming candour about it. Deprived of virtuosity, he relies entirely on his instinct for the telling phrase and the rhythmic felicity and, in the process, reveals an uncomfortable truth about the jazz art – namely that technical experitse is no indication of expressive power. Even Goodman at his best could not improve on Lester feeling his way through *Countless Blues*.

Somewhere along the way, he lost the metal instrument and rarely played the clarinet again.

The intimate circumstances of the Kansas City Six sessions were reproduced at an official Basie recording almost exactly a year later, when a small group from the orchestra recorded for Columbia under the name of the Kansas City Seven. This time the complete Count Basie rhythm section was in attendance, along with Buck Clayton on trumpet, Dickie Wells on trombone and Lester. The two pieces which emerged were *Dickie's Dream* and the simple riff number which came to be regarded as his signature tune, because it bears his name, *Lester Leaps In*.

By sheer luck, Basie's three most powerful soloists played different instruments and possessed musical personalities which complemented each other to perfection: Clayton, forthright and adventurous, Wells with his canny, dry humour and Lester Young in his inimitable prime. *Dickie's Dream* and *Lester Leaps In* are conversations among equals, especially between Lester and Dicke Wells, whose solos seem, in some magical way, to be expressing two sides of the same argument.

As is often the case with the finest Afro-American musicians, music appears merely to be a heightened form of speech, just as the black preacher's discourse hovers tantalisingly between song and declamation. In later years Lester would describe playing a jazz solo as 'telling your story' and insist that, to play a ballad properly, one must know the lyrics as well as the notes. Commentators have puzzled over this remark, but its meaning is perfectly clear: human utterance is an indivisible process, and it is perverse and unnatural to separate its elements into compartments marked 'melody', 'rhythm' and 'words'.

Many years after Lester's death a set of five pieces by the Benny Goodman Septet came to light which contain some of his most delicate playing in the 'chamber jazz' context. The group consists of four Basie men (Lester, Buck Clayton, Jo Jones and Basie himself), Goodman, his bassist Artie Bernstein and the guitarist Charlie Christian. This session, from October 28 1940, was probably a trial run for an idea Goodman had at the time – a small band of soloists playing a slightly more formal version of Commodore-style music. Its greatest significance today is that it brings together Lester Young and Charlie Christian, two players who were obviously made for each other. They have the same cool, unemphatic approach, the same casual fluency and rhythmic poise. Even Christian's tone on the electric guitar bears an uncanny similarity to Lester's tenor saxophone.

35

Flip Phillips, Willie Smith & Lester with JATP, early 1950s
(Melody Maker)

On all five numbers, especially *Ad Lib Blues* and two versions of the same minor-key theme, *Lester's Dream* and *Charlie's Dream*, Lester plays with subdued excitement. The blues, in particular, is magnificent as he uncoils great, serpentine loops of melody over the first four bars of each chorus.

After this encouraging workshop test Goodman established the Septet as a regular alternative to his big band, and it made numerous delightful records over the next couple of years. Unfortunately, Lester wasn't in it, and neither was Buck. There places were taken by Georgie Auld and Cootie Williams respectively. The only other examples we have of Lester and Charlie Christian together are live recordings from John Hammond's 'Spirituals To Swing' concerts of 1938 and 1939. They lack the intimacy of the studio session, but in all other respects they are perfect. Had Christian lived (he died in 1942 at the age of 22), it is more than likely that he would have worked with Lester in later years. His death was a great loss to jazz music.

The voice is an instrument; the instrument is a voice. Nowhere is this fact more vividly illustrated than in the singing of Billie Holiday, juxtaposed with the tenor saxophone of Lester Young. The music they recorded together constitutes a third aspect of Lester's work at his creative peak in the late thirties.

So much reverent critical attention has, quite properly, been devoted to these performances in the intervening years that it is difficult to appreciate that they were originally conceived as what the record industry nowadays calls 'product' – and fairly low-grade, disposable product at that. We owe their existence to two factors, neither of them particularly edifying: the rapid spread of the first generation of juke boxes and the song-plugging system. This is how John Hammond described the matter:

'In 1934, Homer Capehart came out with the first juke box. By 1935, there were a couple of hundred thousand juke boxes in existence. It was as fast as that . . . suddenly all these black bars about the country had juke boxes. I got around enough to realize that their machines didn't have the right material to go in them, so I was able to convince Harry Grey (of Brunswick Records) that it was smart to make the pop tunes of the day acceptable to the black audience. They would be performed without arrangements by the greatest soloists and a superb vocalist. "We can do four sides for 250 to 300 dallars," I added as an inducement. "We'll only need six or seven musicians. The publishers are not going to crack down on us, because you'll already have covered the numbers with Eddie Duchin and Kay Kyser and the rest. They won't squawk if we take a little liberty with the tunes."

'In those days, publishers had complete control over how things should be presented, and if you strayed they would give you a lot of trouble.'

In a back-handed kind of way, this was the perfect recipe for making jazz records, and a flourishing sub-industry soon established itself, with casually assembled bands playing tunes in loosely organised style. Among these were the sessions assembled and led by pianist Teddy Wilson.

These little ad hoc groups contained most of the great soloists of the era, at one time or another, who checked in to earn their $20 whenever the bands they played with regularly happened to be in town. A mere four days after the first recording by the full Basie orchestra, Lester and Buck, Jo Jones, Freddie Greene and Walter Page, turned up at the ABC studios on Fifth Avenue. Also present were Teddy Wilson, Benny Goodman and the 21 year-old Billie Holiday. From the moment of that first meeting, on 25 January 1937, an uncanny sympathy was forged between Billie and Lester. It was an instinctive mutual understanding which went far deeper than a good working relationship; they didn't so much echo each other's thoughts as *think* each other's thoughts, and feel each other's feelings. There are many moments on these records when instrument and voice become one, exquisitely intertwined in a perfect balance of wit and passion.

Billie Holiday is the finest singer in the whole history of jazz. No-one else, save Louis Armstrong, has her flawless timing or tonal delicacy. No other singer has been able to take American popular song and purge it of sentimentality with such clear, uncomplicated, natural phraseology. The wonderful thing about these records is that they were such small-time stuff that she was able to do it unhindered.

Writers of sentimental songs have an unwarranted regard for their own work. It is doubtful whether they appreciated what Billie did to them, if they ever heard her, but they were happy with Eddie Duchin and Kay Kyser and didn't bother to make trouble. The best thing the white entertainment industry ever did for jazz was to leave it alone at this crucial moment.

Remembering these sessions in her autobiography, 'Lady Sings The Blues', Billie wrote:

'I often think about how we used to record in those days. We'd get off the bus after a 500-mile trip, go into the studio with no music, eat nothing but coffee and sandwiches . . .

'I'd say, "What'll we do, two-bar or four-bar intro?" Somebody'd say make it four and a chorus – one, one and a half.

'Then I'd say, "You play behind me the first eight, Lester," and then Harry Edison would come in or Buck Clayton and take the next eight bars. "Jo, you just brush and don't hit the cymbals too much."

'Now with all their damn preparation, complicated arrangements you've got to kiss everybody's behind to get ten minutes to do eight sides in.'

One could take any of the dozens of pieces they recorded by this method and find moments of great beauty, but particularly delectable are two numbers from the session of 15 June 1937: *Me, Myself And I* and *A Sailboat In The Moonlight*. The original songs are so undistinguished, particularly in the lyrics, that it's hard to believe their authors were being serious. In a way, this is part of the charm. No-one, before or since, ever considered either song, so these performances can be heard without the distraction of other people's echoes.

Both pieces follow the pattern which had become standard: introduction, vocal, solos, vocal. *Me, Myself And I* opens with four bars from Lester, then Billie enters, with Buck Clayton tiptoeing along beside her, whispering muted comments. In the background can be heard the unmistakable mumbling sound of two players (Lester and clarinettist Edmond Hall) busking long-note harmonies in that indefinite, keeping-out-of-trouble way that prudent men adopt in such circumstances. For the next chorus Hall plays sixteen bars, Buck plays the middle-eight, pianist Jimmy Sherman the last eight, and then comes the high point – Billie and Lester together.

She may indeed have said, 'You play behind me, Lester,' but that's not what he did. The small, bright voice and the fluent tenor conduct a conversation – half passionate, half kidding – which never palls, no matter how many times one hears it. The two lines are so close that you expect them to trip each other up, but they never do. Neither waits for the other and then follows; they simply move as one. Apart from Armstrong in his prime, there is no more optimistic, spirit-lifting sound in jazz.

A Sailboat In The Moonlight follows a similar pattern, except that there is more of Lester and Billie together. If it doesn't achieve quite the same perfection, that may be because the original song is so weak that even they could raise it only so far. Even so, Billie manages the not inconsiderable feat of suspending disbelief at the lyrics ('A chance to sail away to Sweetheart Bay / Beneath the stars that shine . . .'), and Lester draws phrases from the harmonies far beyond what they deserve.

A few months before this recording Billie had actually joined the Basie band as vocalist, and she and Lester were firm friends. They were not, as Buck Clayton delicately expressed it, 'romantically inclined'; they simply got on well together and their personalities made a perfect match.

Although Lester had been looking out for himself since leaving the family band, he was a shy, unassertive person who tended to take whatever fate decided to dish out to him. Billie, on the other hand, was street-wise, quick tempered and open-hearted. By all accounts she treated Lester rather like a younger brother who needed constant encouragement, although he was six years older. When Lester worried about people criticising his sound it was Billie who said, 'Oh, no, Lester! You have a *beautiful* tone, and you watch – after a while everybody's going to be copying *you*!' (She was right there.) When Lester discovered a rat in his hotel room it was Billie who insisted that he should move in with her and her mother.

Together they smoked prodigious quantities of marajuana and drank a fearsome concoction of their own devising, which they called 'top and bottom' – one half gin and one half port. He called her Lady Day and she called him Prez – short for The President. Billie's mother they called Duchess. The name Prez stuck to him for the rest of his life – and, indeed, beyond.

The giving of names had long been Lester's speciality. Buck Clayton he named 'Cat Eye', Benny Morton was 'Mr Bones', Basie was 'The Holy Man' and Dickie Wells was known for a while as 'Gas Belly' ('Because,' he later explained in injured tones, 'of my troublesome stomach'). The band's road manager, who already laboured under the family name of Snodgrass, became 'Lady Snar'.

Billie stayed with Basie for less than a year, during which time she regularly skinned the musicians in crap games, got the band's pay raised by threatening to leave and take Prez with her, waged constant war with Jimmy Rushing, whom she despised for being parsimonious, and had a small affair with Freddie Greene. Before falling victim to heroin, a few years later, Billie was a buoyant, tough, sparky individual.

JATP, Stolkholm 1952, with Ray Brown, Roy Eldridge, Flip Phillips & Max Roach (Melody Maker)

Lester Young left the Count Basie Orchestra in December 1940. The reason is almost invariably given as Lester's refusal to record on Friday the 13th – an explanation which seems to derive from a news item in the January 1st 1941 issue of 'Down Beat', announcing the split:

'Lester Young and Count Basie, friends and co-workers for the past five years in Basie's band, parted two weeks ago. The split came as a terrific surprise to followers of Basie and the band. Basie said he would rather not comment. Young . . . likewise refused to discuss the change and said he wasn't sure what he would do . . . Les, who failed to show up for a record date on Friday 13th, said "Go 'way and lemme sleep – a man's got no business makin' music on Friday the 13th".'

Now, that reads like the invention of a desperate hack to me. It also shows how close to the surface the old racist stereotypes lurked, even in a supposedly liberal-minded organ like 'Down Beat'. Idle and superstitious darkie. As we have seen, nothing could keep Lester from playing. He could hardly get his clothes on quickly enough when woken with the news of a jam session, and had probably played on every Friday the 13th since the age of ten.

One thing is certain; everyone was remarkably tight-lipped, both at the time and subsequently. Basie always steered majestically away from the subject when it came into view, and when Lester was asked the straight question, 'Why did you leave the Basie Band?' he replied: 'That's some deep question you're asking me now. Skip that one, but I sure could tell you that, but it wouldn't be sporting. I still have nice eyes. I can't go around thinking evil and all that. The thing is still cool with me because I don't bother about nobody . . .' etc, etc.

By implication, Lester denied the Friday the 13th tale soon afterwards anyway. On January 15 1941 a 'Down Beat' news story included these two sentences: 'Don Byas will probably inherit Lester Young's tenor chair. Basie has been using several subs since Young was fired.'

Some weeks later (March 1) the following extraordinary letter appeared in the 'Chords and Dischords' section of the paper: 'To the Editors. May I correct Mr Ed Flynn, who wrote in the Jan 15 'Down Beat' that Lester Young (formerly of Count Basie's orchestra) was fired. My husband was not fired. He quit for reasons of his own. I will appreciate your making this clear. Mrs Lester (Mary) Young.'

As the Fletcher Henderson episode had revealed, Lester had a 'thing' about not being fired. Presumably he had been brooding over the report so much that Mary wrote to the paper in the hope of relieving the tension at home.

Since this is Mary's first, and indeed only, appearance in the story, it is an opportune moment to bring up the somewhat obscure question of Lester's marriages. It is generally agreed that he was married three times, his first and third wives both being named Mary.

Mary One he may have married in Kansas City, but they certainly were not living together at the time Lester moved in with Lady Day and Duchess. Whatever the case, she displayed touching loyalty in writing to 'Down Beat', a loyalty for which she probably received little recompense. Lester was the last man any sensible woman would have chosen as a husband. Brought up on the road, he had no conception of a settled home life and only ever felt at ease in temporary accommodation. His entire worldly possessions consisted of a tenor saxophone, a record player and a few records, and a suitcase of clothes.

The second Mrs Young is a great mystery. It seems that she was white and that she married Lester in California, probably around 1943. The marriage was so short-lived that it hardly counts.

Mary Two, by far the most important to Lester, bore him two children. She figures later in the story.

We don't know for certain why Lester left Basie, but we do know that the band was sailing through some choppy water in 1940. An almighty row had blown up between Basie and MCA, his booking agency, with Basie threatening to break up the band and join Benny Goodman. The agency was reportedly sending the band up to 500 miles on a single one-nighter, failing to book them into locations with direct radio wires (an important thing for a band's exposure), and leaving them loafing around for weeks on end without work. To add to everyone's frustration, Basie kept going off for the odd week as featured guest with Benny Goodman.

Very likely the reason for Lester's going is to be found in this blizzard of ill feeling. Terrified of unpleasantness as he was, he must have found the spectacle of his friends shouting and threatening one another unbearable. There had been disagreements in the past, but on the whole the band had stood together in a tough world. This was different. Constitutionally incapable of joining in the melee, depressed and hopeless, he probably just walked away. He may even have made some gloomy reference to Friday the 13th as he did so. Ironically, a bare month after Lester's departure Basie bought himself out of the MCA deal for $10,000, and the row evaporated.

Thus Lester Young, at the age of 30, found himself a bandleader for the first time. He formed a six-piece combo and took up residence at a New York club called Kelly's Stables. Looked at from the point of view of what is now called Career Development, this was a sound move. A star player, which Lester now was (among aficionados, at any rate), couldn't go on being somebody else's sideman. As a bandleader, his name would be up there on the marquee, in this case replacing that of Coleman Hawkins, who was leaving Kelly's Stables. If Lester had had a press agent he would have made much of the 'Young Master Succeeds Old Master' angle. With his band nicely ensconced in a small but quite prestigious venue, all he needed was a recording contract – which he didn't get. Never one of nature's hustlers, he probably didn't try too hard.

It is infuriating that at this precise moment, 1941, when a profound and disturbing change was about to come over Lester Young's music, the recorded work dries up almost completely. What there is consists of two jam-sessions taken from a WNEW broadcast six days after the fateful Friday the 13th, four numbers by Lester's band accompanying the singer Una Mae Carlisle, a session with Billie Holiday and four numbers with a pickup band called Sammy Price and his Bluesicians.

The jam-session is so badly recorded that it's useless, but the rest have occasional half-choruses and middle-eights by Prez. There are no outstanding Lester performances among them, although Billie Holiday sings so well that he might have done wonders, given more room and less fussy arrangements. Lester's own band, with Shad Collins on trumpet, was obviously capable of far more than it was asked to do in backing Una Mae Carlisle, and you can sense Lester holding back in his solos on *Beautiful Eyes* and *Blitzkrieg Baby*. (The latter must be heard anyway, on account of its extraordinary lyrics: 'Blitzkrieg Baby, you can't bomb me/'Cause I'm pleading neutrality . . .')

Then, in May, Lester packed up and left New York for Los Angeles. There he joined his brother Lee's band at Billy Berg's Club Capri on Pico Boulevard, happy no longer to be a bandleader. Nature never intended him as a leader of men and the whole idea of being in charge of other people appalled him. 'There's always a bastard in the bunch,' he once remarked, 'and you never know who it is.' Now Lee could worry about the bastards.

No two brothers could be less alike. Lee was everything that Lester wasn't – smart, personable, authoritative, business-minded. He even played golf. John Hammond remembered him as 'the perfect member of the black bourgeoisie.' Hammond met Mr Young Senior shortly before the old man died, and told him how much he admired his son. 'Which one?' asked Billy Young. 'Why, Lester.' '*Lester*? Oh, no; the great person in my family is Lee!' Not surprisingly, the brothers were never particularly close friends.

Nevertheless, Lester stayed with Lee Young's Esquires of Rhythm for about a year, and it was in California that he next entered a recording studio. What emerged was startlingly different from anything that had gone before. Accompanied only by Nat King Cole's piano and Red Callender's bass, he plays with a kind of wistful absent-mindedness quite unlike the energetic, youthful sound which had popped like a cork out of the Basie ensemble. With that session of July 15 1942 begins what critics often describe as 'late Lester Young'.

Chapter 3

The lack of recorded evidence from the period between the Spring of 1941 and Summer of 1942 makes this change particularly dramatic. The new tone is heavier, with a certain amount of edge, and the articulation is not quite so sharp. Along with this comes a kind of reflective diffidence in phrasing and far less of the long, flowing line which had been Lester's most notable attribute in the thirties. Since he was still to record some very fine work, one cannot say that these new elements necessarily herald a decline in his powers, but the style that first appears on the Cole/Callender session is undeniably the one he was still employing when his playing *did* decline, towards the end of his life.

Accounting for the change is largely a matter of guesswork. Some critics, probably without bothering to listen to the recorded work in chronological order, solved the problem to their own satisfaction by moving the whole thing forward a few years and blaming it on Lester's army experiences. Once this handy get-out is excluded, one turns first to possible mechanical explanations – reeds, mouthpieces, instruments, recording techniques.

Photographs of Lester taken in the late thirties show him playing two instruments – a silver-plated Conn 'Chu Berry Model' and a Conn 10M, both with a metal mouthpiece, probably by Otto Link. We know that he used to experiment with reeds, particularly when going through one of his periodic fits of nervousness about his sound. ('Oh no, Lester! You have a *beautiful* tone!') In the forties we see him playing a Selmer Balanced Action tenor, an instrument which is mechanically superb, but which doesn't have quite the resonance of the old Conn models. The difference is probably more apparent to the player than to the listener, because the Conn is harder work to play. Lester also changed the metal mouthpiece for one made of Ebonite, a Brilhart 'Ebolin'; its characteristic white plastic inlay is clearly visible in pictures taken around 1943–4. Generally speaking, this gives a thicker sound, but mouthpieces come in a variety of configurations. In 1950 Lester said, 'I always use a plastic reed,' but how far back 'always' referred to is anyone's guess.

No significant advances in recording technique had been made between the Kansas City Six session of 1939 and the Cole/Callender session of 1942. In any case, they both took place in small, cheap studios which are unlikely to have had the latest equipment.

So, apart from some possible minor effect brought about by switching instrument and mouthpiece, we can rule out a purely mechanical explanation.

Reed instruments differ from all the others (except the harmonica and the jew's harp) in that they are actually taken into the player's body. Strings and percussion are operated at a distance, and even brass instruments lie against the outer edges of the lips. The saxophone, being a reed instrument, goes inside the player's mouth, not far (a matter of three quarters of an inch usually), but it is enough to establish a mysterious intimacy.

What goes on inside there? Once the jaws close and the lips form an airtight seal, that sliver of cane and wedge of metal or plastic become a temporary part of the human physiognomy. The diaphragm pushes the lungs, air is expelled, the reed vibrates and its movement resounds in the teeth, the mouth cavity, the intricate labyrinth of sinuses. The most precise and delicate movements a human being can make take place inside the mouth, and there, in that secret place, the saxophone player makes his sound. That is why, as jazz writers are always telling us, the saxophone, of all instruments, most resembles the human voice.

Our voices convey far more than words. They betray our feelings, our age, our confidence or lack of it, even our state of health. They are *us*, physically and spiritually, and the uncanny parallel between voice and instrument extends to this as well.

If Lester Young's sound and phraseology no longer expressed the buoyant optimism of former years it was probably because he no longer *felt* optimistic or buoyant. Away from the orbit of the Basie band with its long-standing friendships and private jokes, away from companions who liked and admired him and understood that his sometimes aloof manner proceeded from shyness and extreme sensitivity, he was at a disadvantage.

There was also the question of ever-present racism to contend with. One of the most telling phrases in his private language was 'I feel a draught', meaning that he detected racial hostility. He had always been particularly susceptible to draughts, and as he got older this susceptibility grew to the proportions of an obsession. Later, he coined a phrase of Jacobean resonance to express it: 'Von Hangman is here!'

The private language sprouted luxuriantly during this period. 'Eyes' meant enthusiasm (as in the song-title *I Only Have Eyes For You*), 'Bells' meant enjoyment (sometimes elided to 'ding-dong'), white musicians were 'grey boys'. It was Prez who first used the term 'bread' for money, as in 'Eyes for the gig, but how does the bread smell?' Pianist Jimmy Rowles, who worked with Lee Young's band in 1942, says, 'It took me about three months to even understand what he was talking about.' Matters were further complicated by the fact that Lester tended to refer to everyone, male or female, as 'Lady' – 'Lady Tate', 'Lady Webster', 'Lady Sweets'.

The Lee Young band remained in California for about 15 months, during which time it teamed up briefly with Slim Gaillard and Slam Stewart, an association which must have borne a marked resemblance to the Tower of Babel, since Gaillard was another great linguistic innovator. Billie Holiday came out to sing at Billy Berg's for a while too, and one can only fume impotently at the lost opportunity of a record session featuring her and Lester at a crucial moment in both their careers.

In August 1942 the group moved to New York to take up a residency at Cafe Society Downtown, before disbanding early in 1943. Lester joined Al Sears and his band for a while, drifted around the 52nd Street clubs and, finally, rejoined Basie in December.

The manner of his rejoining is as peculiar as his leaving. Jo Jones claimed to have run into Lester in a 52nd Street bar one afternoon, bought him a beer and told him: 'Now, don't forget. We're at the Lincoln Hotel. Be at work tonight at seven.' And, at 7pm, there he was.

This seems a very odd way of going about things. Would Basie have taken the stand that night with a four-piece saxophone section, but for this fortuitous meeting? We know that Don Byas (Lester's replacement since January 1941) left Basie in December 1943, and we know that he was a man of uncertain moods and dangerous temper. Possibly he had stormed out, or been thrown out, leaving Basie to hire temporary deputies by the night. Basie may even have asked Jo Jones to go looking for Lester and to assure him that bygones were bygones. He was never a man to harbour grudges.

Whatever the case, Prez – less than three years older, but disconcertingly different from the mildly eccentric young person of 1940 – planted himself quietly behind the music-desk marked 'CB' with the air of one who has come home after a long and testing journey.

As if by magic, the recordings begin again, dozens of titles in less than a year, with a variety of small groups. They prove that the change detectable in the Cole/Callender session was no temporary aberration.

The new furriness in Lester's tone is marked, but by no means unattractive, and there is a laconic note in the phrasing which suits it perfectly. Consciously or not, he has reconstructed his style and emerged poised and eloquent.

As examples of late swing-period playing these records are, without exception, beautiful. No longer in the vanguard, but with their styles fully mature, musicians such as Buck Clayton, Dickie Wells and Bill Coleman perform with magisterial aplomb. They were all, of course more robust personalities than Prez and had emerged into early middle-age full of confidence. Nevertheless, it is his solos which dominate these records. Trumbauer's airy jauntiness has all but evaporated by now, leaving only the wry, ghostly grin of a very hip Cheshire Cat.

There were two sessions in the final month of 1943, the first on December 21st, under the leadership of Dickie Wells, for the Signature label, and the second, exactly a week later, by the Lester Young Quartet, for Keynote. Both companies were small, specialist concerns producing records for keen jazz followers, and they stuck to the same pattern as the 1939 Commodore recordings – informal and loosely organised gatherings of intelligently chosen musicians playing themes which they themselves wanted to play.

The intervening years had not brought any significant change in Dickie Wells' style, except perhaps to see his tone grow riper and more vocal and his imagination more adventurous. Always a perfect partner for Lester he performs here with the grave jocularity which marks all his best work. One can almost feel Lester's relief at being once more in such company as he unfurls solo lines of effortless grace and formidable ingenuity. The youthful suppleness of the late thirties has been replaced by a certain caution, but the incisive musical mind is in full working order, arranging and rearranging phrases, sifting, organising, following a train of thought which seems obvious when expressed, but which no-one else could ever have conceived.

To listen to Lester Young, particularly at this period of his life, is to follow the workings of a supremely elegant mind. It doesn't move with blinding speed, like Parker's, but it moves with absolute justice. It is a mind incapable of concealing itself behind a facade of mannerisms or well-tried formulae. Every solo had to 'tell a story' and the story had to be true, to reflect the feelings of the moment. No other jazz musicians's work has ever been so emotionally transparent, so devoid of rhetorical defences. Lester Young's playing is a window onto his soul: that is what makes it so moving and, as we shall see, the story it tells is ultimately a tragedy.

Among the sessions recorded during the second Basie period, that of 28 December 1943 is particularly fine. It was the first to feature Lester alone, accompanied by the standard piano/bass/drums rhythm section, and the four numbers from it are generally regarded as being among his best work. The first, *Just You, Just Me*, offers an instructive contrast with the youthful *Shoe Shine Swing* in that, whereas that was impetuous and optimistic, this is gentle and ruminative. In *Shoe Shine Swing* one catches only fugitive glimpses of the original theme; *Just You, Just Me* begins with a caressing, sparsely decorated exposition of the melody, from which grows an improvised chorus so clear in outline that it seems simply to be another way of looking at the tune. There is none of the old rhythmic flamboyance, no catch-me-if-you-can, no knowing wink. Instead, he moves with infinite gentleness through the harmonies, approaching their most characteristic points (the E natural of C7, the C flat of A flat minor) from unexpected directions. The most noticeable difference of all is in the pitch of the whole piece. More than half the notes are in the lower register of the instrument, whereas in former times he used this region only as a springboard or turning-place for phrases which found their climax in the upper register. This, combined with the thicker tone, imparts a dark, somewhat rueful quality to the piece. Even so, the phrases are balanced with all the formal rigour of earlier days, and choruses are still squared off neatly with dextrous little movements ending on the keynote.

In this period, too, the slow ballads begin to appear, notably the deeply touching *Ghost Of a Chance*, from April 18 1944. The main motif of this song exploits Lester's favourite interval of the augmented fifth and he imparts to it an overwhelming sadness, rising briefly to a hovering, indefinite ninth. He had never before made much use of chromatic substitutions, but here he inserts one of magnificent eloquence in the eighth bar of the theme-statement, a drooping little phrase composed of E flat, A flat, E flat and D flat over a G7 chord – weary resignation summed up in four notes. There are no official Basie recordings from Lester's second stay with the orchestra. The few broadcast transcriptions and forces' V-Disc records have brief solos by him, although nothing of any great moment. Henceforth his career was to be as a soloist.

The summer of 1944 saw the Basie orchestra in residence at the

Plantation Club in Los Angeles, and it was while they were there that Lester took a prominent part in 'Jammin' The Blues', a ten-minute Warner Brothers film directed by Gjon Mili, a highly regarded photographer who had a great love for jazz music and musicians.

Jazz has, on the whole, not been well treated in the cinema, which is strange, seeing that these are the two art forms in which America is supreme. There are, of course, jazz sequences in some feature-length movies, together with a fair number of shorts and numerous 'soundies', made for a kind of cine-juke-box which enjoyed a brief vogue in the forties. However, 'Jammin' The Blues' is different from any of these. Whereas the others present the music as part of an act, or at least purport to show the musicians playing for an audience, 'Jammin' The Blues' sets out to evoke the atmosphere of an after-hours jam-session. The viewer is placed in the position of an eavesdropper or fly on the wall while the music unfolds. The method is by no means *cinema verité*; each shot is painstakingly set up and lit in the dramatic manner of the period. The soundtrack was recorded separately and the filming took place later, with the result that the alert viewer cannot help noticing the lack of synchronisation as the players' movements fail to match exactly the notes they are supposed to be playing. Neverthless, 'Jammin' The Blues' is a landmark in the presentation of jazz in the cinema and has become perhaps the most celebrated of all jazz films, its only rival being 'St Louis Blues', featuring Bessie Smith. It was certainly the first to treat the art of jazz with any kind of respect, although even that had to be tempered with a certain caution.

Among those taking part in the session was guitarist Barney Kessel, who was (and indeed still is) white; so absolute was the taboo against mixing the races on terms of equality that Kessel appears throughout either in silhouette or heavily shadowed. And here, of course, lies the reason for the cinema's neglect and misrepresentation of jazz. Three years later the feature film 'New Orleans' handed out the most famous indignity of all by casting Billie Holiday as maid to a kind of cut-price Deanna Durbin figure whose name, fortunately, escapes me. Nowadays, when black television detectives of superhuman persistence regularly lug cringing white malefactors off to the chokey, such practices look like the rituals of some remote and hopelessly dim primitive tribe.

But 'Jammin'The Blues' is priceless anyway, simply because it has Lester – withdrawn, watchful, slow-moving, wearing his famous hat, his head tilted to one side to accommodate the 45-degree twist of his mouthpiece. How widely 'Jammin' The Blues' was shown during the mid-forties no-one seems to know, but it established the public image of Lester Young which stuck to him throughout his life and remained after he was gone. The picture in the film fits perfectly with other things – the language, the nomadic existence, the dope, the refusal to get involved. Put this all together and you have the very model for a subcultural type which was to appear a few years later in American society: you have, in short, a hipster.

'Jammin' The Blues' was nominated for an Academy Award in 1945 but Lester was by then beyond the reach of any share in this honour which might have come his way. He was in a place which could have been expressly constructed to conform with his worst imaginings, his own personal Room 101. He was in US Army Detention Barracks, Fort Gordon, Georgia. This is how it happened.

Draft dodging was a moderately simple art in the days before computers and in a country as vast as the United States. All you had to do was keep moving, and that's what musicians did anyway. But if you were a star soloist with a name band, sooner or later they'd get you. And they did – a few days after work on 'Jammin' The Blues' was finished.

As Buddy Tate described it 35 years later, in a 'Melody Maker' interview with Brian Case:

'A lot of musicians beat the Draft by saying, "Well, I didn't get it –I was on the road." We were all trying to stay out, because we were making so much money and there were so many lonely ladies.

'So, the FBI found out where we were going to be. We were playing three months in Watts (ie at the Plantation Club), and this young guy came out one night – zoot suit on, big chain down to the knees like Cab Calloway. He introduced himself, and we thought he was a fan. He stayed all night, and he said, "I'd like for you and Lester and Sweets and Jo to be my guests" – and he bought drinks and drinks and drinks all night.

'At the end, he pulls this badge and shows it to Lester and Jo Jones. "Be at this address at 9 o'clock in the morning, or we'll come and get you and you'll go to jail for five years!"

'It upset Lester. He said, "Goddam it! Ain't that a bitch! The little guy – I liked him. He gained my confidence. I started to turn him on!" I said not to worry, because by this time Lester's drinking a quart of 100 proof a day, and they won't want Jo either, because he's crazy. But man – the next day they put them in.'

54

Lester in the mid-1950s (Melody Maker)

Several people tried to get them out again – among them Basie's manager Milt Ebbens and promotor Norman Granz – but the authorities dismissed the appeals. Everybody tries to get out of it, especially when there's a war on.

First, there was a medical, which revealed that not only was Lester spectacularly unfit and an alcoholic, he also had syphilis. Then came an induction interview, at which Lester, in answer to a routine question about drugs, told the interviewer that he had smoked marajuana daily for the past eleven years. He was quite precise about this. It was, therefore, in the full knowledge of what it was taking on that the US Army accepted him.

Thus, on September 30 1944, a 34 year-old, red-haired, green eyed, alcoholic, syphilitic, pot-smoking, negro tenor saxophone player of no fixed address became 39729502 Private Young, Lester W – enlisted as a warrior.

For the first three months he stumbled along without causing serious injury to himself or anyone else, but on New Year's Day 1945 the trouble began, at Fort McClellan, Alabama. It seems that Lester was going through an obstacle course, and at some point in this Tati-esque performance contrived to fall on his backside. He was carted off to the camp hospital for what is described in the records as 'minor rectal surgery'. It was while he was in hospital that the military phenomenon known as Private 39729502 etc etc was wonderingly inspected by the camp shrink, or Chief of Neuro-Psychology, Dr Luis Perelman, who described Lester as being in a 'consititutional psychopathic state manifested by drug addiction (marajuana, barbiturates), chronic alcoholism and nomadism.' The good doctor could not, however, suggest what might be done about this parcel of afflictions, so he acted like the seasoned soldier he was and passed the buck. He concluded that this was a 'purely disciplinary problem and that disposition should be effected through administrative channels'. So far Lester had not been accused of anything, apart from falling on his behind, so it's difficult to know quite what this 'problem' was supposed to be which might be disposed of by disciplinary means.

Lester was sent back to duty on January 24 and a week later, alerted most likely by Perelman's helpful remarks, the MPs arrested him for possession of marajuana and barbiturates. Another shrink, one Lawrence J. Radice, peered into Lester's psyche and was distressed by what he found therein. To Perelman's list of horrors he added Lester's common-law (white) wife, the brief Second Mrs Young. That, as far as he was concerned, did it. 'In view of his undesirable traits and inadequate personality,' wrote Radice, 'he is unlikely to become a satisfactory soldier.' Buddy Tate could have told him that five months before, but at least the solution seems obvious – let him out again. But when Lester's court martial convened on February 16 it was far too bemused by the spectacle of what it had recruited to be in any fit state to see the obvious.

The details of this whole episode, and particularly of the trial, long a subject of enthusiastic speculation, came to light a few years ago in consequence of the US Freedom of Information Act. They were elicited by John McDonough, Richard M. Sudhalter and Time-Life researcher Ann Holler while preparing the notes for a set of Lester Young albums. The transcript reveals a degree of mutual incomprehension woeful to behold.

Lester's commanding officer, a Captain Stephenson, recounted how a search of the accused's possessions had yielded a quantity of unprescribed pills, two bottles of pink liquid and some home-made cigarettes, all of which were sent for analysis. Lester told Captain Stephenson exactly what he had told the induction interviewer – that he was a musician with Count Basie's band and had been using marajuana for eleven years. The pills he had bought on the base. Characteristically, he was at some pains to assure the officer that he 'never harmed anyone'.

Appearing in his own defence, Lester told the story of his injury and subsequent treatment. This revealed that he had been allowed no period of recuperation:

Q. What did you do when you came out of hospital – go to bed?

A. Sent me out on the field.

Q. Carry a full pack?

A. I don't know. It was a pack and a rifle.

Q. And this was when you immediately returned from the hospital?

A. Yes, sir.

Lester's defending officer asked him about withdrawal effects:

Q. Now if you do not take these drugs, smoke these things, does it affect you in any way physically?

A. Yes, sir, it does. I don't want to do anything. I don't care to blow my horn and I don't care to be around anybody.

Q. Affects you badly?

A. Just nervous.

Q. Could you do this training here if you left them alone?

A. No, sir. because I tried, sir. I tried it, truthfully . . . .

Q. Feel pretty nervous now?

A. I think about it all the time.

It had clearly been wrong to take such a man into the service; he had equally clearly been returned to duty far too soon, but these objections were disallowed. Private Young was sentenced to dishonourable discharge, forfeiture of pay and, most devastatingly, a year's detention in disciplinary barracks. Reviewing the sentence, the Judge Advocate's department admitted that 'his age as well as the nature and duration of his undesirable traits indicate he can be of no value to the service,' adding the ominous phrase, 'without severe disciplinary training.' The sentence, the review concluded, was 'both legal and appropriate.'

Lester served ten months in Fort Gordon. One can only imagine what torture it was for him, a soft, slow-moving man, condemned to a world where everyone shouted and all movement had to be at the double. On one occasion he tried to escape, or rather he hid behind a bush, while out on a working party, and thought about running away. But the guards had guns and this was Georgia – and anyway, he couldn't hide for the rest of his life, not in his profession. So he came out from behind the bush before anyone noticed he was missing.

He was allowed to play, however, at the regular staff dances. Another member of the band was the composer Gil Evans, then a sergeant based at nearby Augusta. He smuggled in an occasional supply of whisky and other comforts. A fellow prisoner was guitarist Fred Lacey, whom Lester rewarded for his friendship by employing him later in his band.

In December 1945 Prez was released with his dishonourable discharge. The Axis powers had been defeated without his aid, and all he could say about the matter was, 'I'm out. That's the only thing that counts.'

It has often been observed that whereas entire bands, such as Glenn Miller's, joined up and carried on pretty much as before, dressed in a different uniform, the great original genius of the swing era wound up in the slammer. But it is doubtful whether Lester would have lasted very long in an army band anyway. There was something about him which simply enraged the kind of people who are put in charge of things. It wasn't just the fact that he seemed incapable of standing up straight or walking in a soldierly manner, it wasn't even the drugs and the drink. The really intolerable thing about Lester was that he wasn't *keen*, couldn't be made keen and couldn't even put up a minimal pretence of *being* keen. His total indifference to all the things that responsible people are supposed to care about – like the future and winning the war and being a credit to the platoon – was a denial of all that the military stood for. These were the 'undesirable traits' that did for 39729502 Private Young, Lester W.

The simple, cartoon-type outline of Lester Young's life, commonly encountered in record sleeve notes and thumbnail histories of jazz, goes something like this: Lester arrived on the scene at the peak of his powers and stayed there, his playing unchanged, until the Army nabbed him. After his release he was a broken man whose music was so changed as to be practically unrecognisable, and through the last fourteen years of his life it declined steadily into drunken incoherence. All this, apart from the opening statement, is in varying degrees untrue.

As we have seen, his tone and phraseology had undergone a transformation in the four years following his first departure from Basie into a less mercurial but still perfectly integrated style. It was the music of an older, more wary, more introspective man. Life in the detention barracks dealt a fearful blow to his dignity and courage, a blow that might indeed, have proved fatal to his art. But, miraculously, it didn't.

By all accounts, he spent the first few months after his discharge wandering about like a lost soul, first in New York and later in Los Angeles, picking up the pieces. During this time he would have discovered that a whole new style of jazz had bubbled to the surface while he had been away. Be-bop was the rising force, its leading figures being Charlie Parker and Dizzy Gillespie. Also he could not help but notice that the young generation of tenor players were, almost without exception, taking *him* as their prime model and adapting *his* style to the configurations of be-bop. This discovery caused him alarm rather than gratification, but more of that anon.

Lester mooched about, taking stock of the scene and recovering his composure, as well as he could, throughout most of 1945, and in October he entered a recording studio once more. The four numbers recorded at this, the first session under his new contract with the Philo label (later to be re-named Aladdin), make complete nonsense of the 'broken man' theory. His technique is sharp, his imagination fully engaged, his tone, if anything, tighter and more controlled than in some of his immediately pre-army recordings. With wry defiance he named the first piece *DB Blues*, after the detention barracks, and based it on his two favourite forms, the blues and *I Got Rhythm*: two blues choruses, the middle eight of *Rhythm* and another blues. A despondent and hopeless man would not have done this; he would have settled for something less risky than a 44-bar cycle with which to announce his return. As far as I know, no-one else had ever tried this particular idea before, although it has occasionally been done since. He creates an effect of lazy nonchalance with his lagging phrases, but there is nothing lazy about the playing on *DB Blues*. It is secure and purposeful, and packed with the surprising twists and turns which mark all his best work. And the ballad from the session, *These Foolish Things*, has a melting elegance that compares more than favourably with *Ghost Of a Chance*, recorded two years earlier.

Less than two months later he is again found in sparkling form at a session with Nat Cole and Buddy Rich which yielded no fewer than eight finished takes. Once more he is poised and confident, pursuing a characteristically devious line of thought and throwing off conversational asides, all with an air of bland innocence. By the end of 1945 the knowledgeable listener, going on the evidence of these two sessions, would have concluded that Prez was back with a vengeance.

Indeed, *DB Blues* was a hit, and not just with jazz buffs either. Its relaxed, late-night atmosphere struck a chord in post-war black California. It summed up in its quiet way a spirit of ease and freedom, of getting mellow in some little dive, of not having to wear uniform and jump out of bed at crack of dawn. For soldiers, eagerly looking forward to the day when they would achieve that most coveted promotion of all – to the rank of ex-serviceman – it was a siren song. There is a version of *DB Blues*, recorded for the black forces' radio show 'Jubilee', in which the announcement of the title brings forth a chorus of rueful chuckles from the studio audience. They may not have known about Lester's experiences in the DB, but they recognised a dedicated ex-serviceman when they heard one.

One effect of his incarceration, however, was obvious to everyone who knew him. His habitual caution with strangers had turned to suspicion and his shy, aloof manner to hooded withdrawal. The mannerisms with which he had always protected himself were magnified to the proportions of a personal Maginot Line. Von Hangman was making increasingly frequent appearances to disturb his fragile tranquillity, and to keep him at bay Lester drank gin and smoked pot and withdrew ever more deeply into himself.

But the process was a gradual one, and there were remissions when he seemed almost his old self. Shortly after the *DB Blues* session he joined Norman Granz's company of touring jazz stars, 'Jazz At The Philharmonic'. A showy, combative enterprise, based on the dubious proposition that the more big names that could be packed into a show the better the results would be, JATP was the worst possible setting for a musician of Lester Young's stamp. Ten years earlier he would have taken it in his stride, but now, with his style growing ever more inward and reflective, this taking turns to come forward and strut one's stuff before a vast, anonymous crowd made a mockery of his art.

Although it was billed as a public jam-session, JATP was nothing of the kind. It was a show. The Kaycee jam-sessions had been contests, but the prize was not the loudest applause. The point of the jam-session was to play better and more intelligently than the other contestants, and the judges were the players themselves and perhaps a tiny gathering of knowledgeable friends. The important thing about the great Hawkins battle had been that Hawkins himself was forced to admit defeat. It is not possible to package this kind of thing and put it on in concert halls, and Lester understood this very well.

He explained on several occasions that the places where he could work most effectively were small clubs and dance halls. Clubs were intimate and relatively quiet and in dance halls the rhythm of the dancers communicated itself to the musicians and inspired them. The fact is that jazz of Lester's kind, the purest and most subtle kind, doesn't actually need a listening audience at all. What it does need is an atmosphere of relaxation. The musicians play; people are present. If they want to listen they draw near and attend, otherwise they can sit at the bar, talk to each other, perhaps get up and dance. When a master is on the stand, and playing well, they'll listen anyway because they will fall under the spell of his music. Perhaps this is an element which jazz has inherited from Africa, where music has always had a functional, social role. Certainly, the idea that the way to experience music is by sitting silent and motionless in a seat is peculiar to Western Europe – and only in comparatively recent times at that.

Whatever the case, Lester's JATP performances are, for the most part, brisk conducted tours through his repertoire of phrases. All the best surviving work of his last fourteen years was done either in studios or in clubs, with someone recording the proceedings. But Granz paid far more than any club owner could ever afford; in his first year with JATP Lester earned $50,000. For the first time in his life he found himself reasonably well-off.

The JATP tours took him to Europe several times, and it is significant that, whereas critics were at best lukewarm about his official performances, people who heard him sitting in at late-night sessions say he played magnificently and with relish. The French critic Charles Delaunay recalled: 'The first time he came over with JATP his short, mediocre appearance disappointed nearly every one of his fans. But pianist Henri Renaud and a few other musicians managed after the concert to take him to the Tabou, where he sat with the local band and really *blew*. 'There we discovered that Lester could still blow when he wanted to, when he was in the proper environment or mood.' After one such night Lester told a friend, 'There are too many people at the concerts and I don't think my music interests them; they've come for something else. I bore them. I prefer to play for those who like my music.' For five consecutive nights Lester sat in with French musicians, playing from 2am until dawn.

As the forties gave way to the fifties, Lester's professional life settled into a three-part routine: touring with JATP, leading his own small band and appearing as visiting soloist at jazz clubs.

In 1948 he got himself a manager, Charlie Carpenter, a one-time songwriter, who looked after his bookings and generally took care of things. He seems to have done an efficient job, given the peculiar nature of his client. Lester's band, which had an on-off existence for almost ten years, caused a certain amount of distress to his old supporters. Its changing personnel was composed mainly of young and fairly inexperienced musicians, with the exception of the trumpeter Jessie Drakes, who was a permanent fixture from 1948. An efficient if somewhat wooden player, Drakes had been installed by Carpenter for the excellent reason that he was a reliable and authoritative man. It was all very well for John Hammond to complain that, whereas Lester had once been surrounded by his peers, he now worked with nonentities. This is to ignore the fact that Lester had only once, and disastrously, been *in charge* of his peers. Left to him, it would have been Kelly's Stables all over again. With Carpenter's management and Drakes acting effectively as leader, Lester Young and his Band was a going concern.

Among the young musicians passing through Lester's band were many who were to become famous themselves. One was Connie Kay, later drummer with the Modern Jazz Quartet, who described the band's way of working to Graham Colombé: 'Lester's was the last regular group I worked with before joining the MJQ, but it wasn't a permanent job. Twice a year he'd cut out and play with Jazz At The Philharmonic, and he'd do a solo, so at that time the band would be laying off. I did a lot of freelancing – record dates, playing in Birdland and with other bands – until Lester came back. Then we'd work a few clubs.

'We never rehearsed anything. He never said anything to me about how I should play, so I guess he was satisfied, because I kept the job. Lester never played more than three choruses on anything. If he played four it was very unusual. There were times when I wanted him to play more, but he wouldn't. He'd always leave you wanting more rather than play all night till you got tired of hearing him.'

Going by its records, the band wasn't anything like the sad travesty it was made out to be, but it wasn't the Kansas City Six or Seven either, and that's what Lester's long-time admirers and colleagues were looking for. Jo Jones was particularly scathing: 'At one time in Lester's life they said, "Lester don't sound like he used to." I said, "Who's he playing with?" . . . How the hell do you think *I* would sound playing with a bunch of high-school kids?'

The fact is, Lester wasn't looking for challenges. He had enough to contend with, defending himself from the world and holding his fragile personality together. So long as the 'kiddies', as he called them, played the rhythm and changes correctly behind him he could get on with the job of expressing his own thoughts and feelings.

At one point the cries of complaint reached such a crescendo that Aladdin Records commissioned Leonard Feather to set up a session in New York featuring Prez with a group of sharp young players of rising reputation: Gene Di Novi, Chuck Wayne, Curley Russell and Tiny Kahn. The idea didn't go down at all well. In the studio Lester muttered a tune title and started blowing. The result, naturally enough, was chaos. They started again, and again, without even a word, Lester launched straight in. Gene Di Novi suggested mildly that it might help if everyone knew what they were supposed to be doing. Lester stared blankly at a point on the wall a couple of feet above Di Novi's head and said wearily, 'If Prez's kiddies were here (he had begun referring to himself in the third person), the kiddies would *know* what do do.'

In the end they managed to get four numbers down and one of them, *East Of The Sun*, is rather a good performance, although Prez deliberately trails off at the end instead of finishing cleanly. It was his protest at being told that his band wasn't good enough.

The young musicians in the band, and those he encountered on his peregrinations as a visiting soloist, were, naturally, playing in the modern style of the day, which was be-bop. One might expect this to have caused him difficulty, but it didn't. On occasion he would grumble about drummers who 'dropped bombs' behind his solos and pianists who filled every corner with substitutions and passing chords, but this was when things were taken to extremes. In the main Prez was perfectly at home with the shape of the rhythm section as it developed through the late forties and early fifties. Indeed, he took the view that his own playing was developing in a new direction too, and was impatient with those who asked him why he no longer played in the style of ten years ago: 'I can't do it. I don't play like that any more. I play different, I live different. This is later; that was then. We change; move on.' This is what exasperated him about the criticism of the kiddies. People were trying to turn him into what he called a 'repeater pencil', turning out facsimiles of his former self which would only be an act. He was incapable of dissembling in this way. Every performance was an act of self-discovery and self-revelation and he could no more go back to the jaunty optimism of 1936 than he could reel in the years and be young again: 'This is later'.

With all this in mind, listening to performances by the band recorded live or taped from the radio during the period 1948–1952 is an instructive as well as enjoyable experience. In the first place, they reveal Lester as being completely at home in the company of young be-bop musicians. The recordings are a bit rudimentary and the band somewhat ragged, but no more so than most other bands of the period caught in live performance. It is the raggedness of excitement. If these recordings remind us of anything it is the Parkers, the Navarros, the Damerons – young men on the crest of the be-bop wave. And Lester is clearly not one of those swing-era players, like Benny Goodman, who added a splash of be-bop to stay in fashion. He is right in the middle of it all. *Be-Bop Boogie*, from the Royal Roost, December 1948, is full of headlong fervour, and a version of *Sunday* from the same session shows Lester juggling accents with immense aplomb over a tempo which plainly gives the kiddies more than a little trouble at times. The tale is repeated often during these years.

In 1948 Lester married for the third time and, with his new wife, Mary, became established in the only permanent home he had ever known, a small house at St Albans, Long Island. A son was born, Lester Jnr (known to all as 'Little Lester'), and later a daughter, Yvette. Mary, according to Leonard Feather, was 'a fragile, proud, introspective woman, the only one who had ever wanted to create a home for him. But she never fully understood him, nor was she able to lead him.'

Nevertheless, Life with the Youngs had all the outward appearance of suburban normality. In the opening paragraph of a 1956 Down Beat interview with Prez, Nat Hentoff presents a picture of Lester as head of the household which is so ordinary as to seem positively bizarre:

'On a recent Saturday afternoon at his home in St Albans, Long Island, Lester Young was alternately watching television and answering questions. Eight year-old Lester Young Jnr had gone to the movies. The pet of the house, a seven year-old Spitz named Concert ("We got him on the day of a concert") was in quizzical attendance. Making coffee was Mary, Lester's wife; also present was the astute, outspoken Charlie Carpenter, Lester's long-time friend who has been with him since 1946 and has been his manager since 1948 . . . '

To Prez this way of life was new and totally unfamiliar. He was now in his forties and had passed his entire existence in that state characterised disapprovingly by the army shrink as 'chronic nomadism'. Just as an English colonial administrator might have continued the habit of a lifetime by dressing for dinner in some tropical outpost, so Lester brought to his new-found role of paterfamilias all the casual profanity of the wandering hipster.

Among his neighbours were two elderly ladies, pillars of the local black church. Sunning themselves one afternoon on their porch they beheld the heart-warming spectacle of Lester and Little Lester throwing a ball to one another in the back yard. After a while they tired of the game and turned to go indoors. Lester tried the handle; the door wouldn't open. The fond father chided his son gently: 'There, you dumb mother-fucker, see what you did? You done shut the door and locked us both out the house!'

Jo Jones encountered Prez pushing Yvette in a baby carriage down a New York street. How did he find coping with the children, in particular their excretory functions? 'Well,' said Lester, 'I don't mind the waterfall, but I can't stand the mustard.'

'You'll see! After a while everybody's going to be copying you!' Billie had said it to cheer him up, but when her prediction came true it brought him no comfort.

In the days when Lester was riding high with the first Basie band his tenor saxophone was heard by millions of people, on records, in person and via the radio. Some of these people were very young, and some of *them* were destined to become musicians. He never suspected it (because who, in the days before teenagers were invented, paid any attention to what kids thought?), but a quite extraordinary number of them were profoundly affected by his music. They were blissfully unaware of the arguments which raged among musicians and older jazz lovers about the novelty of Lester's sound and approach. They just thought it was the most beautiful thing they had ever heard and made up their minds to follow him. Through the years when Lester was playing in Lee's band, through his second Basie period and while he was locked up in the DB, they were growing up, the best of them getting their first jobs in bands. With so many men away in the services jobs were quite easy to come by. When Lester emerged, shaken, from the army there they were, rank upon rank of them, young, bright, devoted. Some were black and some white – Stan Getz, Dexter Gordon, Al Cohn, Wardell Gray, Zoot Sims, Paul Quinichette, Allen Eager. Race and social background made no difference. They were Lester's spiritual children. One of them, Brew Moore, a white boy from Mississippi, where the races still scarcely acknowledged each other's existence, spoke for them all: 'Anyone who doesn't play like Lester is wrong!'

It should have made him happy but it didn't. A less complicated man would have smiled proprietorially at their devotion and even crowed a little over this final proof that he had been right all along. But the whole business just made Lester nervous.

By 1950 it seemed that every young tenor player in the world, in New York and Los Angeles, London and Stockholm, Tokyo and Manila, was aiming at the same pale, glancing effect. They may have got it second-hand, from Getz and Co, but its origin was clear. Apart from Lester, only three men, Armstrong, Parker and Coltrane, have had such a devastating effect on the sound of jazz as it played by musicians at every level of competence. As Lester's sound, mediated particularly through the recordings of Stan Getz, spread in ever widening circles, it entered deep into the fabric not only of jazz but of popular music in general. Whenever a tenor saxophone emerged briefly from the ensemble of a dance band or light orchestra it spoke with the same accent.

But to Lester it was painful, because what these young men were

JATP 1953 tour (Melody Maker)

echoing was his own younger self. Labouring as he was to articulate the emotions of middle age, he must have found the sheer energy of the sleek young men unbearable. To Leonard Feather, in 1950, he admitted grudgingly, 'if you're talking about the grey boys – Allen Eager, he can blow.' And in one ragged live recording by Eager from April 1947, a jam-session broadcast over station WNEW in New York, we can hear what Lester must have heard which caused him such anguish. In his solo on *Sweet Georgia Brown* Eager is young Lester to the very life – poised, relaxed, confident and resourceful. The tone is almost exactly that of *Taxi War Dance*, the articulation so clean and precise that it makes you want to shout aloud with delight. It is the music of a young man, telling his story. To Lester such performances were a cruel, ever-present reminder of his youth. 'They're picking the bones while the body's still warm', he remarked glumly.

Lester's playing had always intimately reflected his life. He didn't resent the young men as an entertainer might resent having his most valuable jokes or songs lifted. It was more that they had appropriated his voice, which was part of him. How could he use it to tell his story when others were using it to tell theirs? 'When they come off and I go on, what can I play? Must I copy *them*?' Booked to play alternate sets with Paul Quinichette, whose sedulous imitation had caused some shallow critic to dub him 'the Vice-Prez', Lester said in desperation, 'I don't know whether to play like me or Lady Q, because he's playing so much like me.' And on being informed that someone or other 'sounds just like you', he asked bleakly, 'Then who am I?'

Instead of flattering him, the imitation left him baffled and confused. He drank even more and his playing became more and more introspective. By 1955 things had got so bad that he had a nervous breakdown and wound up in Bellevue hospital.

Throughout the 1950s, the last decade of his life, Lester was under contract to record for Norman Granz's Clef label. Since he was touring regularly with JATP, it was a sensible arrangement and Granz resisted, in Lester's case, his usual impulse to thrust musicians into bizarre formats – strings, big bands, choirs, collections of soloists with wildly different styles. The majority of Lester's Clef recordings were made with simple piano, bass, drums accompaniment, and they vary quite remarkably. Taken together, the Clef sessions constitute a diary of Lester's ups and downs during this period.

From 1950 we have the beautiful, fragile *Polka Dots And Moonbeams*, in which the tenor saxophone steals tentatively through the theme, absorbed and fascinated by its possibilities. In 1951 we find Lester embarking on *It All Depends On You* with a four-bar introduction of magnificent firmness, only to lose interest half-way through. Teamed with Oscar Peterson in 1952, he achieves a pale eloquence on *There Will Never Be Another You* and rises, in *These Foolish Things*, to the translucent candour which no-one else has ever achieved, and which never quite forsook him, even to the very end.

As the years pass one thing is clear. The really startling phrases are increasingly pieced out by makeweight material – the characteristic triplet decorations and a kind of indecisive shuffling about in the lower register. The ghost of Trumbauer's rip still makes an occasional appearance, transformed into a rising ululation, as if Prez were shaking himself free with a mighty effort. Most noticeable of all, his tone becomes increasingly grainy. This is more evident on the studio sessions than on live recordings, presumably because the close-miking renders it more faithfully. On the Kansas City Six records working close to the microphone had revealed unsuspected warmth and depth in Lester's sound; now the same practice shows just how loose that sound has become. The vibrato at the ends of phrases, once like the slight quivering of a taut string, has turned into a tensionless flap. Perhaps Lester is using a softer reed, which takes less effort. Whatever the case, it imparts a touching vulnerability to his work from 1952 onwards.

Over the couple of years leading up to his nervous breakdown in 1955, Lester's records seem more than ever like despatches from the Front. Sometimes the news is bad, sometimes it is quite good, but morale is clearly slipping.

Two numbers, recorded a year apart for Granz, sum up the general direction. In *Tenderly* (December 11 1953), Lester seems intent on giving Stan Getz a run for his money. He plays the theme in a characteristically allusive and knowing way and, far from losing interest, picks up after the intervening trumpet and piano solos, exactly where he left off, bringing the piece to a beautifully modulated close. Most of the improvisation in *Tenderly* is in the higher register of the instrument – usually a sign that Lester is feeling relaxed and happy.

On the other hand, *Come Rain Or Come Shine*, from December 10 1954, does not bring encouraging news. Apparently sunk in gloom, Lester can scarcely rouse himself to play at all. His notes are only just voiced, his sound quavery, the whole performance a ramshackle,

69

makeshift affair. The plastic reed doesn't help, either. These things have a tendency to retain tiny drops of condensation between the lower surface and the mouthpiece, causing the sizzling sound sometimes called 'frying up'. Lester's later recordings are full of examples, and sometimes he even uses the slight buzz for expressive effect. But here it just hangs around, like radio interference.

The stay in Bellevue seems to have done him good, and Lester joined a JATP tour in Autumn 1955. No doubt it was much like all the others but, years afterwards, it yielded an interesting by-product. Bobby Scott – composer, songwriter, recording director, novelist and once, briefly pop star – was then 18 years old and working as pianist with the Gene Krupa Quartet, also on the bill. Twenty-eight years later Scott wrote a wonderfully intimate little memoir of Prez on that tour, which was published in the Gene Lees Newsletter of September 1983.

As the youngest musician in the troupe, Scott was ignored by the rest, and he found that Lester, too, was largely left alone:

'Even the respect shown him was often perfunctory, and too many musicians seemed merely to suffer him . . . I suffered too, reminded by the musicians in an exquisitely subtle way that at my age I was not entitled to an opinion. I've often thought I came by Lester's friendship as a result. We were both suffered . . .

'His clothes draped his frame. I took it that he'd lost weight and simply couldn't waste time and money playing at being a fashion plate. There was something rumpled, but not dishevelled, about his appearance. His walk, which was more a shuffle than an honest walk, had something Asiatic about it, a reticence to barge in. He sidled. It was in keeping with the side-door quality of his nature . . .

'He was a night person . . . He *entered* the evening. Even the quantity of his words increased as the light of day waned. It was as if he'd climbed a ridge of small hillocks, then settled into a golden period, a span of bewitched time . . . His stick-like body, so worn by his utter disregard for its health, straightened to its limit only during those hours of music. And the music turned on his capacity for cameraderie and humour.'

Lester bestowed the name 'Socks' upon the young pianist (Bobby Scott/Bobby-Socks/Socks) and made him his confidant.

'In a Texas airport he came under the scrutiny of some Texas Rangers.

Lester with Lionel Hampton, Elsie Smith & Eddie Chamblee
(Melody Maker)

They looked at him as if he were a Martian, in his crepe-soled boots and pork-pie hat with the wide brim, forgetting of course their own Western headgear. Prez elbowed me and whispered, "Go tell them I'm a cowboy, Socks!" . . .

'For me, the best moment of each evening was Lester's solo in the Ballad Medley. That year he played *I Didn't Know What Time It Was*. I never became bored with it. I realised that it was his sound production and phrasing that seduced me. And there was, to my ears, a reverent quality that he instilled in the notes. Though he couldn't help but sound laboured and worn, it was the voice of a sage.'

The year 1956 seems to have been a reasonably calm and productive one, and it is neatly bracketed by two sets of recordings – one from January and one from December.

Jo Jones had always maintained that the trouble with Lester was his choice of inferior musicians ('high-school kids') to work with. As we have seen, this was not really true and, anyway, Lester was quite firm about not wanting to engage in constant re-runs of the past. A 1953 season as featured guest-star with Basie at Birdland had been something of a travesty, with Prez going through the motions on *Jumping At The Woodside*, *Every Tub* etc. But the persistent urging to record him with his old colleagues finally persuaded Granz to set up a session for January 12 1956.

Present were Teddy Wilson, Jo Jones and Freddie Greene (to recall the Billie Holiday records as well as Basie days), bassist Gene Ramey, trombonist Vic Dickenson, who had been on the first *DB Blues*, and trumpeter Roy Eldridge, never with Basie but entirely compatible. The resultant album, 'Jazz Giants 56', is quite excellent. Teddy Wilson plays like a dream, the rhythm section swings lithely and the soloists, Lester included, seem inspired by the occasion. On the following day Lester returned to record seven titles with Teddy Wilson and he plays even better, although one can't help noticing the looseness of his sound when heard against such a background. Nevertheless, in the parade of ups and downs this is a decided up.

The December recordings are different in almost every external respect. Prez was working odd weeks as visiting soloist at clubs around the country and December 3 found him opening for six nights at Olivia Davis's Patio Lounge, Washington DC. The resident Bill Potts Trio were to accompany him – three young men just out of the army, at the start of their professional careers. It was a familiar routine for Lester – a brief talk-through with the trio to decide tunes and keys, and then settle down to a night's work. The thing about this gig was that Bill Potts recorded it with professional equipment.

It wasn't until 25 years later that the recordings were finally issued, on four twelve-inch albums, and they are a remarkable document. Lester actually plays better on many of the tunes than he does on 'Jazz Giants 56' – and the version of *These Foolish Things* is stunning. The sound is much firmer, too. It's only a guess, but I think he may have had his saxophone overhauled. He was notoriously bad at looking after his instruments, and the vanishing lower notes on 'Jazz Giants' sound to me like the result of leaking pads. Whatever the case, the Washington records contain some of the best work of Lester's last years, and we can infer from them that he rose to similar heights in other bars and lounges across the United States throughout the period when his studio recordings and JATP performances seem to be telling another story. More great jazz solos have sunk into night club walls than ever found their way to a recording microphone.

In his sleeve-notes to the Washington records Bill Potts makes it quite plain that the young players in the trio held Lester in a degree of respect which bordered on devotion. His account also reveals that, with fellow musicians, black or white, Lester was not the suspicious, withdrawn character that the rest of the world saw:

'I can honestly say that never in my life have I met a more sincere, understanding, considerate, kind and sweet man . . . We had our own band room upstairs and, during intermissions, the four of us would just hang out. Willie, Jim and I would spend most of the time picking Lester's brains, as well as listening to some great stories of the old days. He was such a nice man with a great sense of humour and never said anything unkind about anyone.'

As a kind of visual companion to the Washington records, there is a 'photographic essay' in the 1959 Metronome Year Book, by Herb Snitzer. He followed Prez to a similar gig in New York at around this time and captured very well the atmosphere of one night's work – the backstage conversation, the small, dimly lit room, the complete lack of showbusiness pretension in the whole affair. Lester, the commentary tells us, travelled to and from the club by subway.

The final crack-up began in 1957. Alcoholism and malnutrition put him back in hospital, but this time he didn't seem much better when he came out. He appeared as guest with Basie at the Newport Jazz Festival that summer, barely able to play, and his few recordings during the year are painful to listen to, he sounds so weak and defeated.

Ironically, when he was at his low ebb, he was booked to play in a television programme, 'The Sound Of Jazz' – his second and final appearance on film. It is a brief but desperately moving performance, made the more poignant by the fact that Billie Holiday is there with him. She sings *Fine And Mellow*, and when it comes to Lester's turn he rises slowly from his chair, fixes her with sad, hooded eyes and plays one single chorus of such purity and restraint that the despair contained within it shines like a cold moon through ragged clouds.

Lester had not played the clarinet for years, since losing his old metal instrument, but someone gave him another one at around this time and he turned up with it, unexpectedly, for a session with trumpeters Roy Eldridge and Harry Edison in February 1958. His opening clarinet chorus on *They Can't Take That Away From Me* is the last indisputably great statement of his recorded career. The wraith-like tone is so fragile that notes occasionally fail to make it out of the bell of the instrument, but as a paraphrase of the theme this solo is a masterpiece. Careful, probing, rhythmically elusive and wickedly devious, it is quintessential Lester. One can hear in it all the weary sadness of his latter years, but the immaculate purity of his imagination is undimmed. The other players on the session were in far better shape than Lester, but this last, plaintive gasp of genius drowns all their robust craftsmanship.

Things continued to go from bad to worse. There was a further spell in hospital and, in the Spring of 1958, Lester left Mary and the children and the house in St Albans to move into the Alvin Hotel, at 52nd Street and Broadway – across the road from Birdland.

'It wasn't that the marriage ever really broke up,' said Mary. 'He just wanted to be in New York, where things were happening.' In a perverse, back-to-front kind of way he was seeking comfort, going back to the sort of place which had always really been home to him. He was joined there by Elaine Swain, a young woman who had lived with several other jazz musicians and who was apparently, a devoted companion. She took care of him as well as she could and spent hours listening to him talk, recording his rambling discourse in a series of notebooks which she let no-one else read. Lester would sit staring out of the window, watching people come and go in the street below and particularly through the doors of Birdland, where he had played many times. He took a gloomy interest in the saxophone players as they arrived for a night's work. A phonograph played constantly – records by Frank Sinatra, Dick Haymes, Jo Stafford, – ballads with words. And always he was drinking, straight gin mostly, except when Elaine managed to dilute it with water. He ate practically nothing.

Lester's condition was well known to the New York jazz community, but nobody could think what to do about it. His suspicion had grown to such proportions that he simply shut everyone but Elaine off with hip, evasive small-talk. Marshall Stearns, Professor of English and jazz historian, approached a physician friend and fellow enthusiast, Dr Luther Cloud. If Cloud could gain Lester's confidence he might be able to do something.

So Dr Cloud turned up at the Alvin Hotel and engaged Lester in conversation about music. After several such visits he revealed that he was a doctor and offered to help. 'He accepted it beautifully,' says Cloud. Gradually Lester's gin was replaced by wine, he began to eat and took vitamin pills. Cloud wanted to give him some injections too, but Lester was terrified of needles. It was probably this which protected him from the heroin epidemic which raged around him.

'In six months,' Cloud reported, ' he had added weight, was talking sense, dressing and going outdoors.' On August 27 he crossed the street to Birdland for a birthday party arranged by his friends. He played a set, cut a cake, graciously acknowledged a champagne toast and retired to a ringside table with Elaine, Dr Cloud and a group of musicians. To those who had seen him only a few months before, the change was next to miraculous.

He began working again, although a recording from that year's Newport Jazz Festival reveals him in very poor form musically, his phrases disjointed and his breath obviously short. The tenor saxophone is quite a large instrument and simply to operate it requires a certain minimum level of fitness.

Nevertheless, Lester felt ready to accept the unexpected offer of an eight-week season in Paris. Apart from the money, there was the boost to his self-esteem. Prez was an artist of international stature once more, and he looked forward to the trip. One of the great might-have-beens of jazz is the question: what would have happened if the French offer had never been made? Under the watchful care of Elaine, Dr Cloud, Marshall Stearns and others, would Lester's health have continued to improve and his life resumed its customary shambling, up-and-down course into an indefinite future? But the offer did come and it could not be refused. So he flew off, alone, to Paris in late February 1959.

Once established at the Blue Note Club there, Lester adopted an invariable pattern of life. He would play until the early hours, walk exactly the same route back to his hotel, sleep, wake, drink, maybe eat a little, sit around, walk to the club and begin again. He telephoned Dr Cloud a few times and admitted that he had started drinking again – brandy, Cloud guessed. He also complained that he was feeling a draught. This is highly unlikely, or rather, he may have felt it, but it almost certainly wasn't there. Paris had for decades been favoured by black American jazz musicians specifically because of its lack of racism. Lester also complained about his accompanying trio, a complaint which Americans may have been prepared to believe, but this was unfounded too. The band at the Blue Note consisted of the pianist Rene Urtreger, bassist Pierre Michelot and Christian Garros on drums. They were all excellent players, more than a match for most of the kiddies. A man as hard to please as Miles Davis chose Urtreger to record his soundtrack music to the film 'Lift To The Scaffold'. The only reasonable conclusion one can draw from Lester's remarks is that he was sick, unhappy and blaming the things he had always blamed.

It was during the Paris season that Lester gave an interview to the French journalist François Postif. Most of it is a re-run of the life story he customarily delivered on such occasions (the family band, dumping Bronson's tenor player, the Basie telegram, 'that bitch, Henderson's wife', not telling why he left Basie in 1940, etc), but there is one remark which is not only acute but positively epigramatic: 'They want everybody who's a negro to be an Uncle Tom, or Uncle Remus, or Uncle Sam – and I can't make it!' He had never been submissive (Uncle Tom), or lovably garrulous (Uncle Remus) – and the US Army had cause to know exactly what he thought about Uncle Sam. It is a curious fact that Prez, with his reputation for inscrutability and verbal elision, has never been quoted as saying anything silly. Once the language is decoded, the observations are always thoroughly sensible. His remarks about the best conditions in which to play jazz, about the function of the rhythm section, about the fatal trap of trying to repeat one's past achievements, all are firmly based and shrewdly expressed. And, unlike so many jazz musicians, he never made vast, redundant and half-baked statements about Art.

He had been booked for two months, but barely three weeks into the

Paris in the late 1950s, with Rene Urtreger and Pierre Michelot
(Melody Maker)

Paris gig his strength gave out. He was suffering severe pains in his stomach and was almost too weak to get out of bed. Gathering together his few belongings, he hailed a cab and headed for Orly airport, pausing en route at the American Express office to send a cable to Elaine Swain. By the time his aeroplane took off the pains were practically unbearable and soon he began vomiting blood. The cause was varicose veins in his oesophagus; these had ruptured and were bleeding internally. In 1959 a trans-Atlantic flight took about eight and a half hours and Lester, imprisoned in his seat, bled and suffered all the way. With dreadful irony, the date was Friday, March 13th.

There is some doubt as to whether Elaine met him at Idlewild. Whatever the case, he went straight to his room at the Alvin and his chair by the window, drinking steadily between bouts of sickness. Eventually he lay down on the bed and seemed to go to sleep as the Broadway lights came on. Waking in a drunken stupor, he began moving his fingers weakly and forming his mouth into a saxophone embouchure. Then he fell back. He was dead.

A doctor arrived to confirm the death, and the police soon after that. They took charge of everything of value, pending settlement of the hotel bill: $500 in traveller's cheques, his wallet, his ring, and his voice – a worn and much-repaired Selmer Balanced Action tenor saxophone.

When great men die people remember where they were when they heard the news. Jo Jones was at home, reading the sports page of the paper he had bought in the street outside the Alvin Hotel as Lester was sinking into his final stupor. Dr Cloud was driving home from New Jersey and heard it on his car radio. In places far remote from New York City musicians and lovers of jazz learned of the death without surprise but with a sense of infinite loss. They had followed the faltering tale of the past few years, chronicled in recordings which recounted it all too clearly.

The tragedy of Lester Young's art was that it was entirely true to itself. He had called it 'telling your story', and he told the story with such honesty and candour that even the worst parts were plain for all to hear. A lesser man would have dissembled, put on an act, but 'I try not to be a repeater pencil, you dig?'

Lester Willis Young lies buried at Evergreen Cemetary in the New York borough of Queens. Had he lived to become an elder statesman of jazz he would not have found things much to his liking. One can imagine him, trotted out like some holy relic, performing at one of today's open-air festivals, his sound grotesquely mangled by several thousand watts of amplification. No-one ever told a true story in such circumstances, and to lie was not in his nature.

But such speculations are idle. Lester Young left behind him a volume of recorded work which grows more precious as the years pass, the product of a wonderfully elegant mind contained within the body of a gentle, timid, proud, suffering man.

A Selective Discography

I have based my selections on records generally available at the time of going to press and further listening suggestions follow the main discography. The following abbreviations have been used: (as) alto sax; (b) bass; (bars) baritone sax; (cl) clarinet; (d) drums; (g) guitar; (p) piano; (tb) trombone; (tp) trumpet; (ts) tenor sax; (vcl) vocal; all other instruments given in full. Locations: LA (Los Angeles); NYC (New York City). Issues: (Eu) Europe; (Am) United States of America; (J) Japan. I would like to thank Alan F. Newby for his assistance.

TONY MIDDLETON. *London, August 1984*

JONES-SMITH INCORPORATED
Carl Smith (tp); Lester Young (ts); Count Basie (p); Walter Page (b); Jo Jones (d), Jimmy Rushing (vcl)   *Chicago. October 9, 1936*

C1657-1	SHOE SHINE SWING	CBS (Eu) 88223
C1657-2	SHOE SHINE SWING	,,
C1658-1	EVENIN' vJR	,,
C1659-1	BOOGIE WOOGIE vJR	,,
C1660-1	LADY BE GOOD	,,

In 1936 Count Basie Orchestra with Lester Young began recording for Decca records. Please refer to 'further listening suggestions' following the main discography.

BILLIE HOLIDAY AND HER ORCHESTRA
Buck Clayton (tp); Edmond Hall (cl); Lester Young (ts); James Sherman (p); Freddie Green (g); Walter Page (b); Jo Jones (d); Billie Holiday (vcl).

NYC. June 15, 1937

21249-1	ME MYSELF AND I	CBS (Eu) 88223
21249-2	ME MYSELF AND I	,,
21250-1	A SAILBOAT IN THE MOONLIGHT	,,
21251-1	BORN TO LOVE	,,
21252-1	WITHOUT YOUR LOVE	,,
21252-2	WITHOUT YOUR LOVE	,,

For additional Billie Holiday/Lester Young recordings refer to 'further listening suggestions' following the main discography.

COUNT BASIE AND HIS ORCHESTRA

Ed Lewis, Bobby Moore, Buck Clayton (tp); Dan Minor, George Hunt, Eddie Durham (tb); Earl Warren (as): Lester Young, Herschel Evans (ts); Jack Washington (as, bars); Count Basie (p); Freddie Green (g); Walter Page (b); Jo Jones (d); Billie Holiday, Jimmy Rushing (vcl).   *NYC. June 30, 1937*

MOTEN SWING/SHOUT AND FEEL IT/THE YOU AND ME THAT USED TO BE vJR/THE COUNT STEPS IN/THEY CAN'T TAKE THAT AWAY FROM ME vBH/I'LL ALWAYS BE IN LOVE WITH YOU/WHEN MY DREAMBOAT COMES HOME vJR/SWING BROTHER SWING vBH/ BUGLE BLUES/I GOT RHYTHM   Phontastic (Eu) NOST 7639

Note: the above titles are a radio broadcast from the Savoy Ballroom. For remaining titles refer to June 3, 1938.

COUNT BASIE AND HIS ORCHESTRA

Same as June 30, 1937 except Benny Morton (tb) replaces George Hunt.

November 3, 1937

MOTEN SWING/ONE O'CLOCK JUMP/I CAN'T GET STARTED WITH YOU vBH/STUDY IN BROWN/RHYTHM IN MY NURSERY RHYMES vJR/JOHN'S IDEA/GOOD MORNING BLUES vJR/DINAH vJR   Phontastic (Eu) NOST 7640

Note: the above titles are a radio broadcast from the Meadowbrook Ballroom, New Jersey. For remaining titles refer to July 9, 1938.

COUNT BASIE GROUP

Buck Clayton (tp); Lester Young (ts); Count Basie (p); Freddie Green (g); Walter Page (b); Jo Jones (d); Helen Humes (vcl).   *NYC. June 3, 1938*

'ALLEZ OOP'/BLUES WITH HELEN vHH/I AIN'T GOT NOBODY -1/DON'T BE THAT WAY/ SONG OF THE WANDERER/MORTGAGE STOMP   Phonotastic (Eu) NOST 7639

Note: -1 omit Buck Clayton. For remaining titles refer to June 30, 1937.

KANSAS CITY SIX

Buck Clayton (tp); Lester Young (cl, ts); Eddie Durham (solo g); Freddie Green (g, vcl); Walter Page (b); Jo Jones (d).   *NYC. September 8, 1938*

P23421-1	WAY DOWN YONDER IN NEW ORLEANS	Commodore (Eu) 6.24057
P23421-2	WAY DOWN YONDER IN NEW ORLEANS	"
P23422-1	COUNTLESS BLUES	"
P23422-2	COUNTLESS BLUES	"
P23423-1	THEM THERE EYES vFG	"
P23423-2	THEM THERE EYES vFG	"
P23424-1	I WANT A LITTLE GIRL	"
P23424-2	I WANT A LITTLE GIRL	"
P23425-1	PAGIN' THE DEVIL	"
P23425-2	PAGIN' THE DEVIL	"

Note: other titles on 6.24057 do not feature Lester Young.

COUNT BASIE AND HIS ORCHESTRA

Ed Lewis, Harry Edison, Buck Clayton, Shad Collins (tp); Dan Minor, Benny Morton, Dickie Wells (tb); Earl Warren (as); Lester Young, Herschel Evans (ts); Jack Washington (as, bars); Count Basie (p); Freddie Green (g); Walter Page (b); Jo Jones (d).   *NYC. December 23, 1938*

ONE O'CLOCK JUMP/BLUES WITH LIPS -1/RHYTHM MAN -1   Vogue (Eu) VJD 550

Note: -1 add Hot Lips Page (tp). The above titles are from a concert at Carnegie Hall. For remaining titles refer to December 24, 1939.

KANSAS CITY SIX

Buck Clayton (tp); Lester Young (cl, ts); Charlie Christian (solo g); Freddie Green (g); Walter Page (b); Jo Jones (d). *NYC. December 24, 1939*
WAY DOWN YONDER IN NEW ORLEANS/GOOD MORNING BLUES/PAGIN' THE DEVIL

Vogue (Eu) VJD 550

IDA COX

Buck Clayton (tp); Lester Young (cl, ts); James P. Johnson (p); Freddie Green (g); Walter Page (b); Jo Jones (d); Ida Cox (vcl) *NYC. December 24, 1939*
FOUR DAY CREEP

Vogue (Eu) VJD 550

COUNT BASIE GROUP

Buck Clayton (tp); Lester Young (cl, ts); Count Basie (p); Walter Page (b); Jo Jones (d); Helen Humes (vcl) *NYC. December 24, 1939*
BLUES WITH HELEN vHH/MORTGAGE STOMP/DON'T BE THAT WAY

Vogue (Eu) VJD 550

JAM SESSION

Count Basie Orchestra, with Lester Young; Benny Goodman Sextet; Albert Ammons, Pete Johnson, Meade Lux Lewis. *NYC. December 24, 1939.*
LADY BE GOOD

Vogue (Eu) VJD 550

Note: The above titles are from a concert at Carnegie Hall. For remaining titles refer to December 23, 1938. Other selections on VJD 550 do not include Lester Young.

BENNY GOODMAN OCTET

Buck Clayton (tp); Benny Goodman (cl); Lester Young (ts); Count Basie (p); Charlie Christian, Freddie Green (g); Walter Page (b); Jo Jones (d).

NYC. October 28, 1940

BLUES/I NEVER KNEW/DICKIE'S DREAM (Charlie's dream)/WHOLLY CATS/DICKIE'S DREAM (Lester's dream) Jazz Document (Eu) Va 7997
Note: other titles are by Benny Goodman without Lester Young.

UNA MAE CARLISLE

Shad Collins (tp); Lester Young (ts); Clyde Hart (p); John Collins (g); Nick Fenton (b); Doc West (d); Una Mae Carlisle (vcl). *NYC. March 10, 1941*

62747-1	BLITZKRIEG BABY	RCA (Eu) 741117
62748-1	BEAUTIFUL BABY	,,
62749-1	THERE'LL BE SOME CHANGES MADE	,,
62750-1	IT'S SAD BUT TRUE	,,

Note: other titles on 741117 do not include Lester Young.

LESTER YOUNG-NAT COLE

Lester Young (ts); Nat 'King' Cole (p); Red Callender (b). *LA. July 15, 1942*

VAN 1000	INDIANA	Spotlite (Eu) SPJ 136
VAN 1001	I CAN'T GET STARTED	,,
VAN 1002	TEA FOR TWO	,,
VAN 1003	BODY AND SOUL	,,

Note: some issues of the above session have drums overdubbed and 'extra' music added by tape splicing. Beware! Other titles on SPJ 136 do not feature Lester Young.

DICKIE WELLS AND HIS ORCHESTRA

Bill Coleman (tp); Dickie Wells (tb); Lester Young (ts); Ellis Larkins (p); Freddie
Green (g); Al Hall (b); Jo Jones   *NYC. December 21, 1943*

T19003	I GOT RHYTHM	Doctor Jazz(Eu)ASLP1004
T19004	I'M FER IT TOO	,,
T1919	LINGER AWHILE	,,
T1920	HELLO BABE	,,

Note: other titles on ASLP1004 by Coleman Hawkins.

LESTER YOUNG QUARTET

Lester Young (ts); Johnny Guarnieri (p); Slam Stewart (b); Sidney Catlett (d)
                                                NYC. December 28, 1943

		Mercury (Eu) 6336346, (J) EVER 1021	
HL1-1	JUST YOU JUST ME	,,	,,
HL1-2	JUST YOU JUST ME	,,	,,
HL2-1	I NEVER KNEW	,,	,,
HL2-2	I NEVER KNEW	,,	,,
HL3-1	AFTERNOON OF A BASIE-ITE	,,	,,
HL3-2	AFTERNOON OF A BASIE-ITE	,,	,,
HL4-2	SOMETIMES I'M HAPPY	,,	,,

Note: other titles see March 22, 1944.

KANSAS CITY SEVEN

Buck Clayton (tp); Dickie Wells (tb); Lester Young (ts); Count Basie (p); Freddie
Green (g); Rodney Richardson (b); Jo Jones (d)   *NYC. March 22, 1944*

		Mercury (Eu)6336346	(J) EVER 1021
HL21-2	AFTER THEATRE JUMP	,,	,,
HL22-3	SIX CATS AND A PRINCE	,,	,,
HL23-1	LESTER LEAPS AGAIN -1	,,	,,
HL24-1	DESTINATION KC	,,	,,
HL24-2	DESTINATION KC	,,	,,

Note: -1 omit tp, tb. Other titles refer to December 21, 1943.

KANSAS CITY SIX

Bill Coleman (tp); Dickie Wells (tb); Lester Young (ts); Joe Bushkin (p); John
Simmonds (b); Jo Jones (d).   *NYC. March 28, 1944*

		Commodore (Eu) 6.24292
A4746-1	THREE LITTLE WORDS	,,
A4746-2	THREE LITTLE WORDS	,,
A4746-3	THREE LITTLE WORDS	,,
A4746	THREE LITTLE WORDS	,,
A4747-1	JO-JO	,,
A4747-2	JO-JO	,,
A4747-3	JO-JO	,,
A4747-4	JO-JO	,,
A4748-1	I GOT RHYTHM	,,
A4748-2	I GOT RHYTHM	,,
A4748	I GOT RHYTHM	,,
A4749-1	FOUR O'CLOCK DRAG	,,
A4749-2	FOUR O'CLOCK DRAG	,,
A4749	FOUR O'CLOCK DRAG	,,

EARL WARREN AND HIS ORCHESTRA

Joe Newman, Al Killian, Ed Lewis, Harry Edison (tp); Eli Robinson, Dickie Wells, Ted Donnelly, Lou Taylor (tb); Earl Warren, Jimmy Powell (as); Lester Young, Buddy Tate (ts); Rudy Rutherford (bars); Clyde Hart (p); Freddie Green (g); Rodney Richardson (b); Jo Jones (d). *NYC. April 18, 1944*

S5441-1	CIRCUS IN RHYTHM	Savoy (Am) SJL 2202
S5441-2	CIRCUS IN RHYTHM	,,
S5441-3	CIRCUS IN RHYTHM	,,
S5442-1	POOR LITTLE PLAY THING	,,
S5442-2	POOR LITTLE PLAY THING	,,
S5443-1	TUSH	,,
S5443-2	TUSH	,,

LESTER YOUNG AND HIS ORCHESTRA

Billy Butterfield (tp); Hank D'Amico (cl); Lester Young (ts); Johnny Guarnieri (p); Dexter Hall (b); Cozy Cole (d). *NYC. April 18, 1944*

S5446-1	THESE FOOLISH THINGS	Savoy (Am) SJL 2202
S5447-1	EXERCISE IN SWING	,,
S5447-2	EXERCISE IN SWING	,,
S5447-3	EXERCISE IN SWING	,,
S5447-4	EXERCISE IN SWING	,,
S5448-1	SALUTE TO FATS	,,
S5448-2	SALUTE TO FATS (breakdown)	,,
S5448-3	SALUTE TO FATS	,,
S5448-4	SALUTE TO FATS (breakdown)	,,
S5448-5	SALUTE TO FATS	,,
S5449-1	BASIE ENGLISH	,,
S5449-2	BASIE ENGLISH	,,

LESTER YOUNG QUINTET

Lester Young (ts); Count Basie (p); Freddie Green (g); Rodney Richardson (b); Shadow Wilson (d). *NYC. May 1, 1944*

S5454-1	BLUE LESTER (Lester's blues)	Savoy (Am) SJL 2202
S5455-1	GHOST OF A CHANCE	,,
S5455-2	GHOST OF A CHANCE	,,
S5456-1	INDIANA	,,
S5456-2	INDIANA	,,
S5457-1	JUMP LESTER JUMP (Lester's Savoy jump)	,,

Note: For other titles on SJL 2202 refer June 28, 1949.

JAMMIN' THE BLUES

Harry Edison (tp); Dicky Wells (tb); Lester Young, Illinois Jacquet (ts); Marlow Morris (p); Barney Kessel (g); Red Callender (b); Sidney Catlett (d); Marie Bryant (vcl). *LA. Summer, 1944*

BLUES FOR MARVIN/ONE HOUR vMB   Jazz Archives (US) JA18

omit Dickie Wells, Illinois Jacquet.

MIDNIGHT SYMPHONY/ ON THE SUNNY SIDE OF THE STREET vMB/SWEET GEORGIA BROWN   Jazz Archives (US) JA18

John Simmonds (b), Jo Jones (d) replace Red Callender and Sidney Catlett. Add Buck
Clayton (tp); Illinois Jacquet (ts).   *same date and location*
JAMMIN' THE BLUES   Jazz Archives (US) JA18
Note: All the above titles recorded for the film 'Jammin' the Blues'. Only MIDNIGHT
SYMPHONY, SUNNY SIDE OF THE STREET and JAMMIN' THE BLUES are in the released
print. For other titles on JA18 refer to May/June 1946.

LESTER YOUNG AND HIS BAND
Vic Dickenson (tb); Lester Young (ts); Dodo Marmorosa (p); Freddie Green (g); Red
Callender (b); Henry Tucker Green (d).   *LA. October 1945*
123A   DB BLUES   Aladdin (Eu) 801
123B   LESTER BLOWS AGAIN   ,,
124A   THESE FOOLISH THINGS -1   ,,
124B   JUMPIN' AT MESSNERS   ,,
Note: -1 omit (tb). For other titles on 801 refer January 1946, August 1946.

YOUNG/COLE/RICH TRIO
Lester Young (ts); Nat King Cole (p); Buddy Rich (d).   *LA. December 1945*
348-1   BACK TO THE LAND   Verve (J) 23MJ3102
349-2   I COVER THE WATERFRONT   ,,
350-2   SOMEBODY LOVES ME   ,,
351-1   I FOUND A NEW BABY   ,,
352   THE MAN I LOVE   ,,
353   PEG O' MY HEART   ,,
354   I WANT TO BE HAPPY   ,,
355   MEAN TO ME

LESTER YOUNG AND HIS BAND
Howard McGhee (tp); Vic Dickenson (tb); Willie Smith (as); Lester Young (ts);
Wesley Jones (p); Curtis Counce (b); Johnny Otis (d).   *LA. January 1946*
127A   PAPER MOON   Aladdin (Eu) 801
127B   AFTER YOU'VE GONE -1   ,,
128A   LOVER COME BACK TO ME   ,,
128B   JAMMIN' WITH LESTER
Note: -1 omit (tp), (tb), (as). For other titles on 801 refer October 1945 and August
1946.

**Jazz at the Philharmonic recordings from this period and later are in
'further listening suggestions' following main discography.**

LESTER YOUNG with Nat Cole Trio and Buddy Rich
Lester Young (ts); Nat King Cole (p); Oscar Moore (g); Johnny Miller (b); Buddy
Rich (d)   *LA. April 1946*
THESE FOOLISH THINGS/LESTER LEAPS IN   Spotlite (Eu) SPJ119

LESTER YOUNG QUARTET
Lester Young (ts); Kenny Kersey (p); Billy Hadnott (b); Shadow Wilson (d).
                                                             LA. April 1946
DB BLUES   Spotlite (Eu) SPJ119

JUBILEE ALL STARS

Buck Clayton (tp); Coleman Hawkins, Illinois Jacquet; Lester young (ts); Kenny Kersey (p); Irving Ashby (g); Billy Hadnott (b); Shadow Wilson (d)

LA. April 1946

I GOT RHYTHM/LADY BE GOOD/SWEET GEORGIA BROWN   Spotlite (Eu) SPJ119

Note: other titles on SPJ119 by Coleman Hawkins. The selections are from 'Jubilee' radio broadcasts.

ALL STAR GROUP

Buck Clayton (tp); Coleman Hawkins, Illinois Jacquet, Lester Young (ts); Ken Kersey (p); Al McKibbon (b); J. C. Heard (d).   *NYC. May 27, 1946*

LADY BE GOOD   Jazz Archives (US) JA18

omit Illinois Jacquet.

I CAN'T GET STARTED   Jazz Archives (US) JA18

Joe Guy (tp); Lester Young (ts); Ken Kersey (p); Al McKibbon (b); J. C. Heard (d).

NYC. June 3, 1946

TEA FOR TWO   Jazz Archives (US) JA18

Note: above titles from concerts at Carnegie Hall. For other titles on JA18 refer to 'Jammin' the blues', Summer 1944.

LESTER YOUNG AND HIS BAND

Lester Young (ts); Joe Albany (p); Irving Ashby (g); Red Callender (b); Chico Hamilton (d).   *LA. August 1946*

137A	YOU'RE DRIVING ME CRAZY	Aladdin (Eu) 801
137B	LESTER LEAPS IN	,,
138A	LESTER'S BE-BOP	,,
138B	SHE'S FUNNY THAT WAY	,,

Note: for other titles on 801 refer to October 1945 and January 1946.

LESTER YOUNG AND HIS BAND

Shorty McConnell (tp); Lester Young (ts); Argonne Thornton (p); Fred Lacey (g); Rodney Richardson (b); Lyndell Marshall (d).   *Chicago. February 18, 1947*

46	SUNDAY	Aladdin (Eu) 802
	SM BLUES	,,
	JUMPIN' WITH SYMPHONY SID -1	,,
49	NO EYES BLUES -1	,,
50	SAX-O-RE-BOP	,,
51	ON THE SUNNY SIDE OF THE STREET -1	,,

Note: -1 omit (tp). For other titles on 802 refer to December 1947 and December 1948.

LESTER YOUNG AND HIS BAND

Shorty McConnell (tp); Lester Young (ts); Argonne Thornton (p); Fred Lacey (g); Ted Briscoe (b); Roy Haynes (d)   *NYC. December 28/30, 1947*

122	MOVIN' WITH LESTER	Aladdin (Eu) 802
123	ONE O'CLOCK JUMP	,,
124	JUMPIN' AT THE WOODSIDE	,,
	EASY DOES IT	,,

	JUST COOLING	”
141	I'M CONFESSIN' -1	”
142	LESTER SMOOTHS IT OUT	”

Note: -1 omit tp.

For radio broadcast selections from this period on please refer to 'further listening suggestions' following the main discography.

LESTER YOUNG AND HIS BAND

Lester Young (ts); Gene di Novi (p); Chuck Wayne (g); Curley Russell (b); Tiny Kahn (d).   *NYC. December 29, 1948*

1020	TEA FOR TWO	Aladdin (Eu) 802
1021	EAST OF SUEZ	”
1022	SHEIK OF ARABY	”
1023	SOMETHING TO REMEMBER YOU BY	”

LESTER YOUNG SEXTET

Jesse Drakes (tp); Jerry Elliot (tb); Lester Young (ts); Junior Mance (p); Leroy Jackson (b); Roy Haynes (d).   *NYC. June 28, 1949*

S5240-1	CRAZY OVER JAZZ	Savoy (Am) SJL 2202
S5240-2	CRAZY OVER JAZZ	”
S5240-3	CRAZY OVER JAZZ	”
S5241-1	DING DONG	”
S5241-2	DING DONG	”
S5241-3	DING DONG	”
S5242-1	BLUES 'N' BELLS	”
S5242-2	BLUES 'N' BELLS	”
S5242-3	BLUES 'N' BELLS	”
S5243	JUNE BUG (Lester digs)	”

Note: For other titles on SJL 2202 refer April/May 1944.

LESTER YOUNG QUARTET:

Lester Young (ts); Hank Jones (p); Ray Brown (b); Buddy Rich (d)   *NYC. March 1950*

366	TOO MARVELOUS FOR WORDS	Verve (Eu) MV 2672
367	'DEED I DO	”
368	ENCORE	”
369	POLKA DOTS AND MOONBEAMS	”
370	UP 'N' ADAM	”

Lester Young (ts); John Lewis (ts) Joe Shulman (b); Bill Clarke (d)   *NYC. July, 1950*

430	THREE LITTLE WORDS	Verve (Eu) MV 2672
433	NEENAH	”
434	JEEPERS CREEPERS	”

Lester Young (ts); John Lewis (p); Gene Ramey (b); Jo Jones (d).

NYC. January 16, 1951

483	THOU SWELL	Verve (Eu) MV 2672
485	UNDERCOVER GIRL BLUES	"
486	FRENESI	"
488	LITTLE PEE'S BLUES	"

as previous.
NYC. March 8, 1951

529	A FOGGY DAY	Verve (Eu) MV 2676
530	IN A LITTLE SPANISH TOWN	"
531	LET'S FALL IN LOVE	"
532	DOWN 'N' ADAM	"

LESTER YOUNG QUINTET

Jesse Drakes (tp); Lester Young (ts); Gildo Mahones (p); Gene Ramey (b); Connie Kay (d)
NYC. December 11, 1953

1395	WILLOW WEEP FOR ME -1	Verve (Eu) MV 2676
1396	THIS CAN'T BE LOVE	"
1397	CAN'T WE BE FRIENDS	"
1398	TENDERLY	"
1399	NEW DB BLUES	"
1400	JUMPIN' AT THE WOODSIDE	"
1401	I CAN'T BELIEVE THAT YOU'RE IN LOVE WITH ME -1	"
1402	LADY BE GOOD	"

Note: -1 omit (tp).

LESTER YOUNG AND HIS BAND

Jesse Drakes (tp); Lester Young (ts); Gildo Mahones (p); John Ore (b); Connie Kay (d).
NYC. December 10, 1954

2107	ANOTHER MAMBO	Verve (Eu) MV 2685
2108	COME RAIN OR COME SHINE-1	"
2109	ROSE ROOM	"
2110	SOMBODY LOVES ME	"
2111	KISS ME AGAIN -1	"
2112	IT DON'T MEAN A THING -1	"
2113	I'M IN THE MOOD FOR LOVE	"
2114	BIG TOP BLUES	"

Note: -1 omit (tp).

JAZZ GIANTS 1956

Roy Eldridge (tp); Vic Dickenson (tb); Lester Young (ts); Teddy Wilson (p); Freddie Green (g); Gene Ramey (b); Jo Jones (d)
NYC. January 12 1956

2646-2	I GUESS I'LL HAVE TO CHANGE MY PLAN	Verve (Eu) 2317097
2647-2	I DIDN'T KNOW WHAT TIME IT WAS	"
2648-4	GIGANTIC BLUES	"
2649-2	THIS YEAR'S KISSES	"
2650-2	YOU CAN DEPEND ON ME	"

LESTER YOUNG-TEDDY WILSON

Lester Young (ts); Teddy Wilson (p); Gene Ramey (b); Jo Jones (d)

NYC. January 13, 1956

2657-1	PREZ RETURNS	Verve (Eu) 2304213
2658-1	PRISONER OF LOVE	,,
2659-1	TAKING A CHANCE ON LOVE	,,
2660-1	ALL OF ME	,,
2661-1	LOUISE	,,
2662-2	OUR LOVE IS HERE TO STAY	,,
2663-1	LOVE ME OR LEAVE ME	,,

LESTER YOUNG QUARTET

Lester Young (ts); Bill Potts (p); Norman Williams (b); Jim Lucht (d).

Washington, DC. December 1956

A FOGGY DAY/WHEN YOU'RE SMILING/I CAN'T GET STARTED/FAST B FLAT BLUES/ DB BLUES/TEA FOR TWO/JEEPERS CREEPERS   Pablo live (Eu) 2308219

LESTER LEAPS IN/THESE FOOLISH THINGS/I'M CONFESSIN'/THREE LITTLE WORDS/ JUMPIN' WITH SYMPHONY SID/ALMOST LIKE BEING IN LOVE/LULLABY OF BIRDLAND
Pablo live (Eu) 2308225

JUST YOU, JUST ME/SOMETIMES I'M HAPPY/UP 'N' ADAM/INDIANA/G's IF YOU PLEASE/ THERE'LL NEVER BE ANOTHER YOU   Pablo live (Eu) 2308228

TALK OF THE TOWN/I COVER THE WATERFRONT/PENNIES FROM HEAVEN/G's IF YOU PLEASE/ALMOST LIKE BEING IN LOVE/DB BLUES/I'M CONFESSIN' THAT I LOVE YOU
Pablo live (Eu) 2308230

Note: the above titles were recorded at Olivia Davis' Patio lounge.

LESTER YOUNG AND HIS ORCHESTRA

Roy Eldridge, Harry Edison (tp); Lester Young (cl, ts); Hank Jones (p); Herb Ellis (g); George Duvivier (b); Mickey Sheen (d)   *NYC. February 8, 1958*

21929	ROMPING	Verve (Eu) 2304487
21930	GYPSY IN MY SOUL	,,
21931	PLEASE DON'T TALK ABOUT ME WHEN I'M GONE	,,
21932	THEY CAN'T TAKE THAT AWAY FROM ME	,,
21933	SALUTE TO BENNY	,,

LESTER YOUNG QUINTET

Lester Young (ts); Rene Urtreger (p); Jimmy Gourley (g); Jamil Nasser (b); Kenny Clarke (d).   *Paris, France. March 4, 1959*

I DIDN'T KNOW WHAT TIME IT WAS/OH LADY BE GOOD/ALMOST LIKE BEING IN LOVE/ THREE LITTLE WORDS/I COVER THE WATERFRONT/I CAN'T GET STARTED/INDIANA/ PENNIES FROM HEAVEN/ NEW DB BLUES/LULLABY OF BIRDLAND/THERE'LL NEVER BE ANOTHER YOU/TEA FOR TWO   Verve (Eu) MV2698

The following titles are also cited in the text.

FRANKIE TRUMBAUER AND HIS ORCHESTRA

Bix Beiderbecke (cornet); Frankie Trumbauer (c-melody sax); Bill Rank (tb); Jimmy Dorsey (cl, as); Paul Mertz (p); Eddie Lang (g); Chauncey Morehouse (d).

NYC. February 4, 1927

W80393B   SINGIN' THE BLUES   The Golden Age (Eu) GX2513

GX2513 titled The Golden Age of Bix Beiderbecke – 1927

WNEW SATURDAY NIGHT SWING SESSION

Fats Navarro (tp); Bill Harris (tb); Charlie Ventura, Allen Eager (ts); Ralph Burns (p); Al Valente (g); Chubby Jackson (b); Max Roach (d)   *NYC. April 12, 1947*

SWEET GEORGIA BROWN   Spotlite (Eu)SPJ144

PJ144 titled Jazz Off the Air   Vol 1.

Title List of LPs in Main Discography

88223	Lester Young Story – Vol 1
NOST 7639	Lester Amadeus!
NOST 7640	Basic Basie
6.24057	Kansas City Six and Five 1938
VJD 550	Spirituals to Swing
741117	The Greatest of the Small Bands – Vol 3
Va7997	The Rehearsal Sessions Benny Goodman 1940
SPJ 136	Nat King Cole meets the Master Saxes
ASLP1004	Classic Tenors
EVER1021	Prez on Keynote
6336346	Prez at his very best
6.24292	A Complete Session
SJL 2202	Pres/The Complete Savoy Recordings
JA18	Jammin' with Lester
Aladdin 801	The Complete Aladdin Sessions Vol 1
Aladdin 802	The Complete Aladdin Sessions Vol 2
SPJ119	Coleman Hawkins/Lester Young
23MJ3102	The Lester Young Trio
MV2672	Pres
MV2676	Lester's Here
MV2685	It Don't Mean a Thing If It 'Aint Got That Swing
2317097	Jazz Giants 1956
2304213	Pres and Teddy
2308219	Lester Young in Washington DC 1956
2308225	Lester Young in Washington DC 1956 Vol 2
2308228	Lester Young in Washington DC 1956 Vol 3
2308230	Lester Young in Washington DC 1956 Vol 4
2304487	Laughin' to Keep from Cryin'
MV2698	Lester Young in Paris

Further Listening Suggestions

COUNT BASIE AND HIS ORCHESTRA

Ed Lewis, Bobby Moore, Buck Clayton (tp); Dan Minor, George Hunt (tb); Eddie Durham (tb, g); Earl Warren (as); Lester Young, Herschel Evans (ts); Jack Washington (as, bars); Count Basie (p); Freddie Green (g); Walter Page (b); Jo Jones (d)

NYC. July 7, 1937

62334A   JOHN'S IDEA   Affinity (Eu) AFS 1010

Benny Morton (tb) replaces George Hunt

NYC. August 9, 1937

62513A   TIME OUT   Affinity (Eu) AFS 1010
62514A   TOPSY   "

as previous.

NYC. October 13, 1937

62683A   OUT OF THE WINDOW   Affinity (Eu) AFS 1010

Harry Edison (tp) replaces Bobby Moore, add Jimmy Rushing (vcl).

NYC. February 16, 1938

63286A   SENT FOR YOU YESTERDAY vJR   Affinity (Eu) AFS 1010
63287A   EVERY TUB   "
63289A   SWINGIN' THE BLUES   "

as previous

NYC. June 6, 1938

63919A   BLUE AND SENTIMENTAL   Affinity (Eu) AFS 1010
63920A   DOGGIN' AROUND   "

Dickie Wells (tb) replaces Eddie Durham.

NYC. August 22, 1938

64473A   TEXAS SHUFFLE   Affinity (Eu) AFS 1010
64474A   JUMPIN' AT THE WOODSIDE   "

as previous.

NYC. November 16, 1938

64747A   SHORTY GEORGE   Affinity (Eu) AFS 1010
64750A   PANASSIE STOMP   "

COUNT BASIE AND HIS SEXTET

Shad Collins (tp); Lester Young (ts); Count Basie (p); Freddie Green (g); Walter Page (b); Jo Jones (d); Jimmy Rushing (vcl)

NYC. February 2, 1939

64978A   YOU CAN DEPEND ON ME   Affinity (Eu) AFS 1010

COUNT BASIE AND HIS ORCHESTRA

Same as November 16, 1938 except Chu Berry (ts) replaces Herschel Evans.

NYC. February 1939

64982A	JIVE AT FIVE	Affinity (Eu) AFS 1010
64985A	LADY BE GOOD	"

NB: Title of AFS 1010 SWINGIN' THE BLUES

Count Basie complete Decca recordings in chronological order 1937–1939. Four LP Box set. MCA (Eu) 510167 to 510170. COUNT BASIE 'EARLY COUNT'.

Double LP of Decca recordings 1937–1939. MCA (Am) 2-4050. THE BEST OF COUNT BASIE.

All known Count Basie Columbia recordings, including alternate takes. Two 10 LP Box sets. CBS (Eu) 66101. THE COMPLETE COUNT BASIE Vol 1 to 10. 1936–1941. CBS (Eu) 66102. THE COMPLETE COUNT BASIE Vol 11 to 20. 1941–1951.

A radio broadcast from Southland ballroom, Boston February 20, 1940, comprises one side of Jazz Society (Eu) AA512. COUNT BASIE 1940/1944.

Billie Holiday/Lester Young. Double LPs. CBS (Eu) 68228. THE BILLIE HOLIDAY STORY Vol 1. CBS (Eu) 68229. THE BILLIE HOLIDAY STORY Vol 2. CBS (Eu) 68230. THE BILLIE HOLIDAY STORY Vol 3.

Five excellent double LPs issued in the late seventies but currently (August 1984) unavailable, containing most Lester/Billie recordings plus selections with Count Basie. The series producer Mike Brooks has included a most entertaining set of sleeve notes with quotes from Lester Young and many of his contemporaries.

CBS (Eu) 88223. THE LESTER YOUNG STORY Vol 1. JONES-SMITH & WILSON HOLIDAY, INC.

CBS (Eu) 88263. THE LESTER YOUNG STORY Vol 2. A MUSICAL ROMANCE.
CBS (Eu) 88266. THE LESTER YOUNG STORY Vol 3. ENTER THE COUNT.
CBS (Eu) 88267. THE LESTER YOUNG STORY Vol 4. LESTER LEAPS IN.
CBS (Eu) 88268. THE LESTER YOUNG STORY Vol 5. EVENING OF A BASIEITE

Lester Young recordings with JATP. Three LP set includes 1946 and 1949 concert excerpts Verve (Eu) MV 9070–72. JATP – 1940s. Three LP set includes 1952, 1953 and 1955 recordings Verve (Eu) MV 9073–75. JATP – 1950s. A double LP including the 1946 concert recordings Verve (Eu) 2610020. JATP 1944–46. A double LP containing the 1946 recordings. Verve (Eu) 2610024. JATP 1946 Vol 2. Verve (Eu) VRV2 – The Trumpet Battle 1952. Verve (Eu) VRV5 – Bird & Pres Carnegie Hall 1949.

LESTER YOUNG AND HIS BAND

Kai Winding (tb); Allan Eager, Lester Young (ts); Hank Jones (p); Ray Brown (b); Roy Haynes (d); Ella Fitzgerald (vcl). *NYC. November 27, 1948*
HOW HIGH THE MOON Affinity (Eu) AFFD 80

Jesse Drakes (tp); Ted Kelly (tb); Lester Young (ts); Freddy Jefferson (p); Tex Briscoe (b); Roy Haynes (d). *same date and venue*
LESTER LEAPS IN/GHOST OF A CHANCE/SWEET GEORGIA BROWN/JUST YOU, JUST ME Affinity (Eu) AFFD 80

as previous. *NYC. December 6, 1948*
I'M CONFESSIN'/I COVER THE WATERFRONT Affinity (Eu) AFFD 80

Jerry Elliott (tb) and Junior Mance (p) replace Ted Kelly and Freddy Jefferson.
NYC. March 19, 1949
BE BOP BOOGIE/DB BLUES/THESE FOOLISH THINGS Affinity (Eu) AFFD 80

as previous. *NYC. March 26, 1949*
LAVENDER BLUE/LESTER LEAPS AGAIN (Lester leaps in) Affinity (Eu) AFFD 80

as previous. *NYC. April 9, 1949*
MEAN TO ME Affinity (Eu) AFFD 80

Lester Young (ts); John Lewis (p); Gene Ramey (b); Jo Jones (d).
NYC. January 1, 1951
UP 'N' AT 'EM/BACK HOME IN INDIANA/TOO MARVELLOUS FOR WORDS
Affinity (Eu) AFFD 80

as previous. *NYC. January 20, 1951*
NEENAH Affinity (Eu) AFFD 80
Note: all titles on this double LP are radio broadcasts from Royal Roost or Birdland clubs. Title LESTER LEAPS AGAIN.